Better Safe Than Sued—

Jack Crabtree

D0169981

Loveland, Colorado

■ ■

The information contained in this book has been gleaned from years of experience in youth ministry but in no way prepares the reader for every situation. In addition, laws change and vary by jurisdiction. Consequently, neither Jack Crabtree, the Livingstone Corporation, nor Group Publishing, Inc., shall be held liable for any damages that might arise after reading this book.

■ ■

Better Safe Than Sued

Credits
Book Acquisitions Editor: Bob Buller
Chief Creative Officer: Joani Schultz
Creative Development Editor: Dave Thornton
Copy Editor: Helen Turnbull
Art Director: Ray Tollison
Cover Art Director: Jeff A. Storm
Computer Graphic Artist: Randy Kady
Cover Designer: Diana Walters
Cover Illustrator: Lori Osiecki
Production Manager: Gingar Kunkel

Library of Congress Cataloging-in-Publication Data
Crabtree, Jack 1949-
    Better safe than sued / [Jack Crabtree].
        p.   cm.
    Includes index.
    ISBN 0-7644-2053-4
    1. Church group work with youth. 2. Safety education.
    3. Accidents--Prevention. 4. Liability (Law)--United States-
-Popular works. I. Title.
    BV4447.C73 1998
    259'.23--dc21   98-9995
                                                                   CIP

10 9 8 7 6 5 4 3   07 06 05 04 03 02 01 00
Printed in the United States of America.
Visit our Web site: www.grouppublishing.com

Contents

■ ■

Introduction

■ ■

Here's what you should know about this book:

1. All the Stories Are True! What you read in the following pages really happened to me or one of the many youth leaders who were interviewed for this book. Some of the stories are clearly identified with a real name and place. I did change the names and disguised the nonessential circumstances of some of the stories to maintain the privacy (and sometimes avoid embarrassment!) of those who contributed to this book. When just a first name is given, the name used is fictional and is not even slightly related to the real name.

2. I'm a Violator! I'm no safety nut. You won't catch me wearing safety goggles and carrying a clipboard with ninety-nine safety checkpoints. When the pages ahead sound preachy, remember I'm a fellow sinner in safety matters (other matters, too). I'm guilty of laziness, procrastination, ego, fear, overconfidence, and all the other basic reasons we let safety slide. Preparing this material has reminded me repeatedly about how generous God has been to protect the students under my leadership when I have been poorly prepared to guard their well-being. I have a few months head start on you, but we both have a lot of improving to do to protect the health and safety of our young people.

3. This Book Is Not Complete! No doubt you have learned or will learn additional safety lessons not included in these pages. In areas of first aid, insurance, liability, legal requirements, sexual abuse, and so on, I did my best to touch just the high points. There is so much for you to learn in each of these areas. During the next few years, I believe the subject of safety and negligence in our churches will be a growing concern to all of us. I hope each of you will go much further than this book can take you.

4. I Had Plenty of Help! My sincere thanks goes to many people who provided much needed assistance and encouragement to this project. Special thanks to: Dave Veerman, Jim Galvin, and Bruce Barton of Livingstone, who conceived this idea, gave me an opportunity to develop it, and patiently guided me through the process; Claudia Gerwin, who did a zillion phone interviews with youth leaders all across the country; and Michael Kendrick, whose phone calls always spurred my work.

Thanks to youth leaders and camp directors who told us their stories and shared the safety lessons they have learned: Ed Ahlum, Bob Arnold, Tim Atkins, Francis Bartley, Clarence Boland, Bob Borman, Mike Collison, Charlene Cosman, Geoff Cragg, Ken Cragg, Jon Dennis, Byron Emmert, Willie Foote, Jim Green, Betty Ham, Bill Housley, Greg Makin, Mark Miller, Greg Monaco, Mark Oestricher, Jerry Petillon, Terry Prisk, Kaaren Rexroth, John Richmond, Gary Schulte, Joel Smith, Tedd Smith, Peter Vanacore, David Wager, and Bob Kobielush, president of Christian Camping International.

Thanks to the professionals from the fields of law, counseling, social work, and insurance who discussed safety issues with me from their professional experiences: Dick Armstrong, Laura Barnes, John Helfrich, Joseph Infranco, Jim Jensen, Herb Nichols, Dennis Morosco, James Murphy, and Jim Trump.

Special thanks to Becky, my wonderful wife, for her diligent proofreading, candid comments, and steadfast love to me; and to Andy and Ben, my teenage sons, who give me many reasons to smile!

P.S. If you have a youth ministry safety story to tell or if this book has provoked any change in the way you do youth ministry, drop me a note. I've still got plenty to learn.

> Jack Crabtree
> Long Island YFC
> Box 55
> Deer Park, NY 11729

"He who trusts in himself is a fool, but he who walks in wisdom is kept safe" **(Proverbs 28:26).**

Dedication This book is dedicated to Jack and Mary Lu Masterson and their family. Thank you for the unconditional love and support you have shown to me and the Youth for Christ staff.

ONE

This Shouldn't Have Happened...

■ ■

The bad news had been delivered. It was a no-win situation. Larry, a twenty-eight-year-old youth pastor, stood in the doorway halfway between the church van full of teenagers and the desk in the canoe outfitter's shop. In all the planning for this trip, he had never even considered this problem.

He stared at the swollen river 150 feet across the parking lot. How was he supposed to know that this was the weekend the water was released into the river from the reservoir? What was he going to do: run the river or drive this van home?

The owner of the outfitter's shop had said that only experienced canoeists had any business being on the river today. That warning was inside Larry's head, fighting with the fact that they had driven three hours hauling a rack of six canoes for this special one-day outing. The van rocked from side to side with the pent up energy of teenagers psyched for a wild day running the river. Larry felt the pressure building.

Five minutes later, Larry pulled the van and trailer into a parking lot a mile down the road from the outfitter's shop. He asked his crew of church teenagers how many of them had canoeing experience. Only the hand of his volunteer leader went up to join his. Then, with a look of resignation and a slight laugh, Larry shouted, "What are we waiting for?"

Within minutes of hitting the river, almost every canoe had capsized. Everyone was soaked and shivering in the frigid, fast-moving current. It was going to be an adventure.

Larry: Awesome Youth Leader or Stupid Fool?

Several months later, the youth group was still retelling stories of how they ran the river. Most memorable and laughable was Patty, who was so wet and cold that she had turned blue and couldn't breathe. She was shivering so much she didn't have enough strength to get out of the water and back into the canoe. It wasn't until later that night at home that she was able to get warm.

A parent overheard the conversations of the young people and approached Larry privately to express his concern. He asked Larry if he had recognized Patty's symptoms as clear signs of hypothermia and suggested that Patty could have lost her life that day in the river. He questioned Larry's choice to canoe, given the condition of the river that day and the inexperience of the young people.

Larry deflected the parent's concern, reminding him that no one had gotten hurt. More important was the fact that the teenagers had had a great time. Adventure and a few risks make the youth group exciting and more attractive to the nonchurched teenagers who attend. Driving home would have hurt the positive image of the youth group. Larry added that he was confident God would protect them from any real danger because people in the church pray for the youth ministry. It would have been a big mistake if he had driven home without going in the river.

Larry continued his youth ministry without giving another thought to the incident. Most of the students in the youth group still think Larry is an awesome youth leader. Fortunately, for Patty's sake, Larry didn't learn his safety lesson the hard way. Unfortunately, Larry hasn't learned his safety lesson at all. He just keeps rolling along.

Don't think badly of Larry. He does care about his students and would never want to see any of them hurt. But to him, discussion of safety concerns is boring. It stifles the freedom and fun he promotes in the youth ministry activities. Safety warnings sound restricting and probably would squash the excitement and spontaneous fun the youth group is supposed to have.

Larry can't even picture himself standing before his youth group reading off a list of safety regulations. Nothing would destroy the atmosphere of his group as fast as a safety lecture. It would make him sound like a parent. Fear and caution are signs of "thinking old." Larry prides himself in "thinking young."

Larry's attitude toward safety issues reflects the attitudes and practices of many youth ministry workers—both paid employees of churches or organizations and volunteers. Safety is one of the last concerns discussed when youth activities are planned and implemented.

What If Patty Had Died?

But consider the consequences of a different outcome of Patty's time in that chilly river. Suppose the hypothermia had advanced a few more degrees. Patty would have stopped breathing, and her heart would have stopped beating. How prepared was Larry to respond to this life-or-death crisis?

Imagine that the best efforts of the ambulance team and the hospital were not enough to save Patty's life. How would it affect all the people involved?

1. Grief, sorrow, and shock would ravage the youth group and the church.

2. Heartbreak and deep sadness would hammer her

family, her boyfriend, and her best friends. They would cry out to God, asking why such a fine young woman had died before reaching the fulfilling years of her life.

3. Eventually, anger and blame would be leveled at Larry and the volunteer leader. The story of raising hands in the van would become public knowledge. People would second-guess Larry and condemn his decision to canoe the river.

4. Strong love-hate feelings would surface in the youth group. In one sense, the tragedy would give them reason to draw closer to each other with deeper feelings than ever before. However, the painful memories of Patty's death would make it hard to be together without that experience being foremost in their minds. It is likely that many members would seek escape and reduce their involvement.

5. Personal guilt would weigh heavily on Larry, the volunteer leader, and any student or adult who felt responsible for what had happened to Patty. Larry's personal effectiveness and work habits would likely suffer for an extended period of time. He would find it hard to concentrate for any length of time; his thoughts would keep returning to what had happened that day on the river.

6. Within a month, the church leadership would conduct some kind of review concerning the accident. Larry's leadership and his present effectiveness would be closely reviewed. Parents would voice their concerns about safety issues in all aspects of the youth program. Larry's status would be diminished in the eyes of the church leaders and the parents of the students involved.

7. In all likelihood, Larry and the church could expect some type of lawsuit related to Patty's death. The proceedings would continue for several years. The litigation would create rifts between all the people involved. The whole tragic story would be retold many times during the judicial process. There would be plenty of hard feelings between the parties involved regarding the issues of responsibility,

pain, negligence, and money. This day on the river, it seems, would never go away.

8. No one would come out of this chain of events untouched. Everyone would be changed. Relationships would change. Attitudes would change. The personal Christian faith of some would grow stronger; others, their faith shaken, would fall away from their commitment to Christ and the church.

9. One constant would remain. Patty would be gone. What had happened couldn't be undone.

For years, Larry would re-examine his motives for taking Patty and the group into the river on that fateful day. He would have to admit to himself that he had never thought about the possibility of someone dying that day. When he made his decision, he was thinking about wasting a three-hour van ride and listening to the complaints of students who would question his status as an "awesome" leader.

Eventually, Larry might have thought of an alternative plan he could have used that day. Unfortunately, on the day of the accident, those thoughts never crossed his mind.

Of course Larry's attention to safety issues would have been changed forever. He would have learned the safety lesson from the most severe teacher: tragic experience.

Changing Attitudes Toward Safety

Interviews with many youth workers reveal a number of reasons their attitudes toward safety issues changed. They were asked to complete the sentence, "I never took safety seriously until..." Their responses include the following:

"I got older and had children of my own."

"I saw a student in my group get seriously hurt."

"A friend in youth ministry was involved in a horrible lawsuit over an accident involving the youth group."

"Some parents asked me why I hadn't done something

to stop the game in which a student was seriously hurt."

"My board of advisors talked to me about our legal liability."

"After a close call in which we escaped serious injury, I realized how careless we had been."

"I got hurt during a retreat."

Youth workers who have learned the importance of safety in the ministry also identify five major reasons they were previously unconcerned.

1. I was young. Young people feel indestructible. They believe that nothing can hurt them. Challenges are to be taken, not analyzed.

The younger the youth worker, the less likely he or she is to be adequately concerned about safety. Young leaders don't have to give up their enthusiasm and energy, but when they face safety issues, they must force themselves to think like a person who has lived a few more years than the kids in their group.

2. I didn't have children of my own. Parents seem overly cautious and careful until a young leader becomes a parent. Having a child sharpens a person's awareness of danger and safety. One important role of a parent is to think ahead and anticipate any potentially harmful situations. Parents "childproof" a room to keep children from encountering what could possibly hurt them. Responsible youth leaders think the same way as they prepare for youth meetings. It's a mind-set more naturally embraced by a parent who daily looks after his or her own children.

3. I wanted kids to like me. No youth leader wants to spend every activity or trip saying no to the kids in the group. Not wanting to offend or drive away a young person, youth leaders are sometimes afraid to confront students involved in dangerous activities. But the mature youth leader knows that students are not offended when they are confronted in a personal, affirming way. Students don't want to be yelled at or condemned in front of their peers, but they generally appreciate a respectful call to responsibility and maturity.

4. I couldn't afford it. Preparing to operate a safety-conscious youth ministry costs time and money. Unfortunately, most youth workers run their programs on last-minute schedules, either because they are procrastinators or because they are volunteers pressed for time. They rarely consider safety issues. All too often events and activities are planned with no thought given to the potential dangers present. Safety requires training in specific subjects such as first aid, water safety, and emergency procedures. This requires a significant time commitment. How many youth leaders are willing to invest the time and money for such training?

5. I had no experience. A few trips to the hospital emergency room or visits to the hospital room of a student injured during a youth group activity will change a leader's attitude toward safety. Nothing beats firsthand knowledge. Unfortunately, it is a painful and costly method of learning. Leaders can gain wisdom by watching others and heeding the warnings and advice of those who have paid the price of actual experience. Pride and stubbornness, however, keep some leaders from learning by any other means than their own failures. It's a heavy price to pay.

Carrying Precious Cargo

Bob had an eye-opening experience during his first year as youth minister for the church. "I was driving a vanload of students from my church to Youth for Christ's D.C. '91. Just outside of Washington D.C., I noticed the brakes were almost totally gone. I pushed the brake pedal all the way to the floor with little response.

"We were already late, so I took it real slow and nursed the van the last ten miles to the downtown convention center. We arrived safely, and I thought of myself as a hero for getting us through that tough spot.

"A year later I wonder how I could have been so stupid. I had no idea what the terrain of the road or the traffic would be. I could have easily gotten the van into the situation in which only a crash would have stopped us.

"I realize now that my response to that crisis matches the way I have handled personal car problems during my life. The difference is this time was that I was no longer responsible just for myself. I had thirteen kids who belonged to someone else under my supervision and protection.

"I now know that when I operate as youth minister, I must do what parents and the church would want me to do, not what I personally feel comfortable doing."

Bob has undergone a key attitude transformation in his youth ministry. Now he is aware that, in addition to his important job of communicating the Christian message to young people, he is also responsible for providing a safe, responsible environment. His role as youth minister requires him to answer to several important groups of people who will hold him accountable for his decisions.

Youth leaders must be able to give satisfactory answers to the key questions from the people who have put their trust in them as they work with their kids.

The parents want to know:
- Are you protecting my children from danger and harm?
- Do you model a responsible lifestyle for my kids?
- Are you teaching my kids to make good decisions?
- Do you think through all the activities before you ask my son or daughter to participate?

■ Do you love my kids enough to say no to them when it is necessary?

The sponsoring church/organization wants to know:

■ Are you being an ambassador for Christ to everyone involved by showing care and concern for each person's safety?

■ Will your actions bring sorrow to people under our care?

■ Are you teaching and modeling maturity to our youth?

■ Are you exposing us to any unwise liability?

■ Will you bring us any bad publicity?

The participating students want to know:

■ Will you carelessly hurt my friends?

■ Will you pressure me to take chances I cannot handle?

■ Are you concerned about my future?

■ Will I be haunted by sad memories of a careless accident?

The insurance carrier wants to know:

■ Is our contract with your group a wise investment?

■ Will you follow the rules and restrictions we specify?

■ Will you do your job as our partner in protecting these young people?

Imagine that you are our friend, Larry, the awesome youth leader. If Patty had died that day in the river, how would you answer these questions? Say the answers out loud so you can hear how they will sound to the ears of those who will ask the questions. Don't skip ahead! Try to answer for Larry all the questions these people will ask him.

If it is hard to find the right words, make a promise to yourself never to let careless planning or thoughtless decisions put you in that position. Use all the information in this book to reform your youth ministry into an operation that is both fun and safe. Commit yourself to giving your students thrilling memories and a lifetime relationship with Jesus, while protecting their physical well-being.

Fun or Safety?

For most youth ministries, fun is the primary drawing card that gets students to attend. Not many kids are attracted to a youth group because it is safe. It would seem that any group emphasizing safety will appear boring and can expect a drop in attendance.

Just consider the connotations that "fun" and "safe" carry for most young people and their leaders.

Fun means...	Safety means...
saying yes to kids	saying no to kids
kids like the leader	leader unpopular with kids
risk, danger, excitement	rules, caution, boredom
yes—go for it!	no—don't try it!
never being bored	never being alone
freedom	supervision
funny stories to tell	oppressive adult presence
spontaneity	worry and paranoia
living by faith	fearfulness

Many youth workers falsely assume that being safe means not having much fun. Deep in their minds, they believe that if they decide to run a safe youth program, it probably won't be fun or an effective way to reach kids today.

Surprisingly, safe programs can still be plenty of fun. It does take planning and recruiting more qualified people to make plans both fun and safe. On the other hand, the leader can be confident that the fun won't come to an abrupt halt because of a serious injury that could have been prevented with proper planning.

Of course, you can do the best possible job of planning events and protecting kids and still see students injured or even killed. There are many forces beyond your control. You are responsible, however, to recognize the forces you do control and make them safe for the young people you love.

TWO

How Safe Is Your Youth Ministry?

■ ■

It's Friday night. You're the adult leader of the church youth ministry. To give your students something positive to do this night, you decide to open the church gym and youth room. No program. No planning. No problems. Right?

The lights are on. The basketballs are bouncing in the gym. The television and VCR are playing in the youth room. Teenagers are scattered throughout the lighted sections of the church. You opened the church at 7 p.m. and will use your key to close it up at 11:30 p.m. Everything seems fine.

Stop and think! What potential risks or dangers await a youth leader who is simply trying to help teenagers by opening the church for a night of recreation and hanging out? Here's a list of some of the potentially dangerous situations that might occur during this "harmless" night of youth activity at the church. Check the floor plan of the church (p. 18) and the appropriate numbers linked with the potential problems.

Risk 1: You are alone. None of the other volunteer leaders could make it tonight. What would you do if a student needed emergency transportation home or to the hospital? Since no other adult is present, are you vulnerable to a false accusation of abuse by a student? Who would take charge if *you* were injured tonight?

Risk 2: Open door policy. The kids in your group can walk in and out without asking your permission. You have no written record of who is actually here. Two blocks away is a pizza parlor where kids like to go for a quick snack. You have never had someone leave and not come back. Will tonight be any different?

Risk 3: Excitement in the parking lot. Kids rush out

Church Map

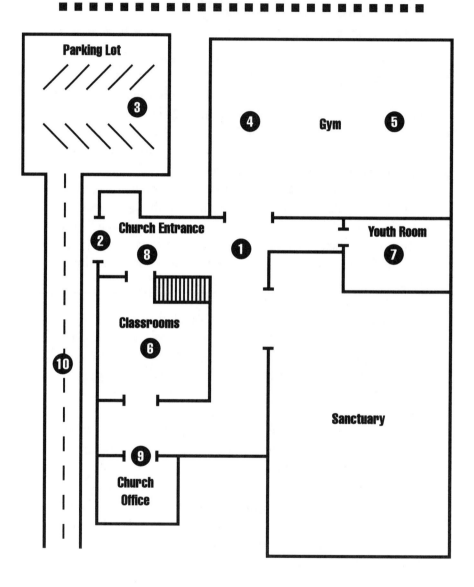

Parking Lot

3

Gym

4 **5**

Church Entrance

2

8

1

Youth Room

7

Classrooms

6

10

Sanctuary

9

Church Office

The Top Ten Safety Sins of Youth Ministry

■ ■ ■ ■ ■ ■ ■ ■ ■ ■ ■ ■ ■ ■ ■ ■ ■ ■

1. Not enough staff

2. Too many kids in the vehicle

3. No time to plan for safety

4. No plan of action to respond to an emergency

5. Students driving

6. No use of seat belts

7. No first aid training or supplies

8. Inadequate paperwork (proper permission/medical forms)

9. Letting a dangerous activity continue (afraid to stop it)

10. Lack of careful supervision (letting kids wander or play around with equipment)

Which of these safety sins are present in your youth ministry?

■ ■ ■ ■ ■ ■ ■ ■ ■ ■ ■ ■ ■ ■ ■ ■ ■ ■ ■ ■

to the parking lot to see another student's new car. You can hear the motor revving and the short squeal of the tires. You can see a car driving in circles while other kids sit on the hood. Should you step outside and play the meanie?

Risk 4: Action in the gym. The basketball game is only half court, but kids are playing hard. You notice that the protective mat for the wall under the backboard is missing. Along one side of the court sit several rectangular tables with metal protected edges—left from the ladies luncheon. You know you would hear plenty of groaning if you stopped the game to fix all these potential dangers.

Risk 5: Michael Jordan wannabes. At the other end of the court, some kids are trying to dunk the basketball by running toward the basket and jumping off a metal folding chair. The chair moves each time they try to dunk. Although they're falling on the floor, they're all laughing hysterically. You will have a hard time convincing them that somebody could get hurt.

Risk 6: Young lovers. You have two steady boy-girl couples who are always hanging on to each other. Where are they now? Are they in the youth room watching videos, or have they wandered down a dark hallway into another area of the church? Should you go looking for them?

Risk 7: The videotape. The television tube is the only light in the youth room. It's hard to see who is bunched into the couches staring at the screen. One of the students brought the video. You can hear the gunfire and some of the bad language. Should you monitor what they watch on these nights?

Risk 8: The ride home. A cute tenth-grade girl informs you she is leaving with some friends who will take her home. Who are these "friends" holding car keys in their hands? You've never seen them before. When did they arrive? You know that questioning her about all this will make her feel uncomfortable in front of these friends. She assures you her parents won't mind. Should you let her go?

Risk 9: Who you gonna call? There is a telephone in the church office. Unfortunately, the office door is locked, and you don't have that key. If someone were seriously hurt, how would you call for help? If you did get help or had to go to the hospital, would you be able to get the student treated if you couldn't reach the parents? After all, you didn't get permission slips or release forms for this activity.

Risk 10: The drive home. What if you drive some of the kids home tonight? Is your insurance coverage sufficient to cover the medical and liability costs for a carload of teenagers if you're involved in an accident? What should you do if the last person in the car is a young person of the opposite sex? What if someone spreads a rumor about your romantic involvement with a student or if a student accuses you of a sexual advance; what recourse or protection would you have?

Should We Always Be Afraid?

Should the "risk list" make you permanently paranoid? The list of possible risks is endless. Do you consider this a ridiculous attack of fearful speculation, or is there an element of hidden (but real) risk every time you offer a youth ministry event?

All of us live with risks and dangers every day. Just driving a car reminds us how close we come to serious injury or death. Just a few inches or seconds often means the difference between life and death. Most of us have to admit that we have been fortunate when we have had lapses in our driving safety. Nothing serious happened. However, if we ignore these little safety "wake-up calls," eventually we will pay for it.

The risk of being a youth leader in North America has increased greatly over the past fifteen years. While the value of each young life has remained priceless, the legal and monetary damages involved have skyrocketed. The youth leader who overlooks the crucial role of safety in his or her ministry risks substantial losses in ministry opportunities, relationships, reputation, time, and money.

Becoming a Student of Safety

Most likely you weren't selected to be a leader in youth ministry because you had a reputation for being safety conscious. You were selected because kids like you or because you know how to have a good time while communicating the gospel. But everyone connected with your youth ministry is quietly counting on you to run a safe program and take care of their kids.

It's OK to admit that safety is not one of your major concerns or strengths as a leader. The mere fact that you are reading this shows your willingness to learn how you can grow as a youth leader who understands safety concerns.

Let's be honest. Safety is a background concern. It's like

being an offensive lineman in football. No one notices anything you do until a defensive player gets by you to slam
the quarterback into the ground. Then all eyes focus on
you, and everyone asks why you didn't do your job. Learn
this lesson now. People will seldom discuss safety with you
until something goes wrong or someone gets hurt.
Unfortunately, learning your lesson then won't get a kid out
of a wheelchair or bring someone back from the grave.

Everyone assumes that your youth ministry is safe. The
people who hired you and kids' parents assume you will be
safe and will not hurt any of their young people. The students assume nothing bad will ever happen to them or their
friends. You assume that God is with you and will protect
you from harm. But safety is too important simply to be assumed. Safety must be built into your youth ministry. But
how do you do it?

Requirements for Students of Safety

First, a youth leader needs to be committed personally
to safety. How will *you* be transformed into a safety-
conscious person? Will it start with the fear of liability or the
fear of what you would tell a parent whose child was seriously injured or killed while under your supervision? Fear *is*
a powerful motivator, but youth leaders should take safety
measures primarily because they have a strong love for all
the students involved.

You don't want to see anyone get hurt, so you need to
invest the time to think ahead and to plan a response to
possible dangerous situations. It takes initiative. It's proac-
tive, not reactive. This investment also requires money and
people. The student of safety rejects the shortcut approach.
It is worth the money to purchase quality equipment and
hire skilled people to provide expertise for training and
medical response.

Second, the student of safety is constantly improving his or her ability to assess risk and danger. That ability is gained only through experience. You can learn vicariously by reading the true stories in this book and listening to others. Or you can learn through real-life experiences, packing away knowledge for future use every time you lead a youth activity or trip. You hope and pray to learn all the vital safety lessons without seeing young people lose their health or their lives.

Developing this risk-assessment skill is like learning to drive a car. If you're smart, you start cautiously, learning to control and stop the car. The fools and the reckless hit the accelerator and think about how to stop safely only when it is too late and the damage is done. It is not a sin to err on the side of caution. Every activity and event you lead should broaden your safety and ministry experience and equip you for more demanding opportunities.

Principles of Safety

The remaining chapters of this book provide specific examples and guidelines for common youth ministry experiences. No book can address all the situations you will face, but every student of safety can master the following general safety principles and apply them in varied settings.

1. The higher the risk, the greater the supervision required. Match your supervision level to the type of activity you're leading. Weekly meetings in the church youth room may require a 1-to-15 adult leader-to-student ratio, but a weekend hike in the wilderness probably needs a 1-to-4 ratio. Raking leaves at the home of a senior citizen may require a 1-to-10 ratio, while handing out bag lunches to the homeless in an inner city setting may call for a 1-to-2 ratio.

2. What is dangerous? Get a clue! The exclusions of coverage by your insurance company provide a general guideline for what the underwriters consider dangerous.

Photographs, slides, and videos can get you into trouble if you aren't careful. All the pictures taken at your events and activities are the property of the youth ministry. However, if you plan to use any of the photographs, slides, videos, or audio tapes in a public setting or in a promotional piece for the youth ministry, you should have a written consent and release form from every person whose picture will be used. (See sample release statement in the appendix on page 230.)

Most liability policies currently exclude snowmobiling, white-water rafting, water balloon launching, and mud bowls. Those exclusions are made on the basis of previous accidents. Obviously, activities that involve motorized vehicles, slippery surfaces, heavy physical contact, turbulent water, and hitting people with any type of projectile merit special attention before you decide to proceed with your plans.

3. There's a big difference between perceived danger and actual danger. You can keep the atmosphere of fun and excitement in your youth program if you sponsor activities that look and feel dangerous but that are, in fact, quite safe. A ropes course (walking a single wire twenty feet off the ground) is both terrifying and thrilling to most kids. In reality, the ever-present safety lines and high quality supervision of a well-maintained and well-run ropes course makes this one of the safest experiences a young person can have. On the other hand, most adults and students feel relaxed and complacent about safety around water when, in fact, the danger is much higher than they might suspect.

4. Plan for the worst-case scenario. Prior to an event, discuss potential problem situations. For example, as you train counselors and drivers for the winter retreat, ask them what they would do if their van (with ten students aboard) was separated from the rest of the caravan and developed engine problems. If they were ten miles from the nearest town, it was nighttime, and it was five degrees above zero, how would they handle the situation? Or when you train leaders for your summer bike trip, ask what would they do if they realized they had made a wrong turn on the route and were ten miles from the destination. What should they do if it's almost dark? Help them think through the options and prepare them to make decisions when the real-life events occur.

That Fateful Day
■ ■ ■ ■ ■ ■ ■ ■ ■ ■ ■ ■ ■ ■ ■ ■ ■ ■ ■ ■

Alan had the world's greatest job. Here he was in his mid-twenties playing basketball in a small church gym with a group of guys from his YFC/Campus Life club. Spending time building relationships with these guys was what his supervisor wanted him to do.

He broke loose from his man and bolted toward the basket. On the way, he tripped over the foot of another player, lost his balance, stumbled, and then crashed into the unpadded wall underneath the backboard. He lay on the floor motionless while the teenage guys stared at him in shock.

Today Alan is living a productive life as an inner city worker for the Presbyterian church, but when he moves, he does it in a wheelchair. He has been paralyzed since that fateful day of basketball.

If you had come to a gym to play basketball or a similar game and saw no padded protective mats on the walls, what decision would you have made?
■ ■ ■ ■ ■ ■ ■ ■ ■ ■ ■ ■ ■ ■ ■ ■ ■ ■ ■ ■

---

5. Learn to recognize the initial signs of danger.
Great athletes have the ability to anticipate what their opponents are going to do next. Responding more quickly than their foes can act, they gain the victory. The safety-smart youth leader anticipates danger. If kids are chicken-fighting (riding on each other's shoulders) in the small swimming pool, can you see the probable landing spot for the head of

How Safe Is Your Youth Ministry? **25**

the student riding on top when he or she falls? What are the signs of young people becoming angry during a competitive game and possibly using excessive force during the next round? Recognizing the initial signs of danger gives the youth leader the advantage and opportunity to intervene before the accident happens.

6. Keep in mind the special needs of your group. Learn to make safety decisions according to the particular needs of the kids in your group. If you take your group on a Follow the Leader exercise through the park, you may jump over a wrought iron fence without realizing that down the line is an overweight student who could be injured trying to get over the fence. Likewise, pitting smaller junior high kids against senior highers in a game with heavy physical contact usually brings trouble.

7. Test it first. Bring your great idea to life with a simulated run, using your staff as "crash test dummies." As you play, you will be able to identify the danger points and modify your idea before you present it to the youth group.

8. Resist the shortcuts. Recognize the forces that pressure you to short-circuit your safety plans. When you are running late, you will tend to skip checking the fluids in the van or the connections on the ropes course. People will forget permission slips, first aid kits, and other important safety matters. Don't let their "problem" pressure you to break the important rules of safety.

9. Make the most of your mistakes. Learn from your mistakes and from the mistakes of others. Sometimes minor accidents and near misses are funny. But don't just laugh about them. Learn your lesson and believe that next time you might not be so fortunate.

10. Take the "my kid" test. Treat each young person like your own child. Don't put any student into a situation in which you would not readily place your own child.

11. Lead by example. The leader sets the pace for

volunteers in the issues of safety and every other matter in youth ministry. Don't bend the rules for your personal comfort or convenience.

12. Balance your theology. Pray for God's protection, but exercise the thoughtful responsibility God has given to you. Don't count on God to suspend the forces of nature or the laws of physics to protect you (or your kids) from the results of careless planning.

To create a safe youth ministry, teach and model these general safety principles to your team of volunteer youth workers. Share experiences that illustrate these principles, and discuss how they apply to your group.

Wake Up and Smell the Coffee!

All youth leaders need to do an honest, thorough assessment of safety issues in their ministry to protect themselves, the reputation of their church or youth organization, and the well-being of the kids and parents who they love and serve. To help you focus on the vital safety issues in your youth ministry, take a few moments to answer the following questions.

How Safe Is Your Youth Ministry?

Volunteer Leaders

Yes	No	Sometimes	
❏	❏	❏	Have my volunteer leaders gone through an application and acceptance process (that includes written applications, reference forms, background checks, and interviews)?
❏	❏	❏	Have my volunteer leaders been screened for any prior criminal, sexual, or physical abuse accusations or violations?

❑	❑	❑	Have my volunteer leaders been trained for the job I have asked them to do?
❑	❑	❑	Have I trained volunteers in general safety procedures, and do I discuss specific safety procedures with them prior to an activity or event?
❑	❑	❑	Do my volunteers understand and practice our prescribed standard of "safe conduct" with students to avoid any suspicion of sexual misconduct?
❑	❑	❑	Do my volunteers know their specific jobs at the events they attend?
❑	❑	❑	Do I have an appropriate adult-student ratio at every event?

Student Information

Yes	No	Sometimes	
❑	❑	❑	Do I have a permission/release form and medical form signed by parent(s) for each participating student?
❑	❑	❑	Do I have current phone numbers so I can contact parents in case of an emergency?
❑	❑	❑	Are parents fully informed (in writing) about the activities in which their children will be involved?
❑	❑	❑	If I have to take any student to the hospital, am I prepared to answer questions I will be asked about personal information, medical information, and insurance?

First Aid and Emergency Response

Yes	No	Sometimes	
❑	❑	❑	Are members of my youth ministry team trained in a certified first aid course?
❑	❑	❑	Is a person trained in first aid present at all of our youth activities and trips?
❑	❑	❑	Is our first aid kit adequately stocked and available at all of our youth activities and trips?
❑	❑	❑	Do I carry with me phone numbers of people who should be contacted in the case of an emergency (ambulance, police, ministry supervisor, parents)?

Drivers and Vehicles

Yes	No	Sometimes	
❑	❑	❑	Do we have a written policy regarding driving standards and who is allowed to drive for all the activities and trips?
❑	❑	❑	Do we only use drivers who are qualified and responsible?
❑	❑	❑	Do we prohibit students from driving other students to our activities?
❑	❑	❑	Do we require the use of seat belts at all times?
❑	❑	❑	Do we regularly check for safety the vehicles we use, including fluids, brakes, tires, and the like?

Planning and Preparedness

Yes	No	Sometimes	
❏	❏	❏	Do we have a clear written set of basic safety rules for the activities of our youth ministry?
❏	❏	❏	Do we have sufficient insurance coverage for both leaders and kids in our youth ministry?
❏	❏	❏	While preparing for an event, do I inspect the physical facilities or location and look for any safety hazards?
❏	❏	❏	To prepare for an event, do I walk through the proposed activities to anticipate what risks are involved?
❏	❏	❏	Do I think through a worst-case scenario to identify potential problems and to plan responses to those problems?
❏	❏	❏	When an activity seems dangerous, do I have the wisdom and courage to stop it regardless of the reaction of the students involved?

Analysis: Each "no" or "sometimes" answer needs your attention. Review these questions and answers with your supervisors and your volunteer staff. Then decide together what you can do to improve the protection you provide for the students in your youth ministry.

THREE

Are You Protected?

■ ■

"Young man, how many times has your outfit been sued?" The county policeman's voice was gruff as his eyes locked on mine.

"None, sir," I answered timidly.

"Well, you ought to consider yourself real lucky based on what I can see of how you operate," he replied, returning to his clipboard and the paperwork for our emergency call.

The policeman had responded to our call for help when a young woman complained of severe head pains and dizziness after hitting her head during a game with four hundred teenagers in the county park. The police officer had arrived minutes before the ambulance and had handled our situation skillfully. We, however, had not won his approval with our unprofessional preparation.

We had answered almost all of his questions about this young woman by saying, "I don't know" or "I'll ask if someone here knows." We had no parental release form, health history form, or information about how to contact her parents. Our activity was just a one-day, four-hour event with students from all the Campus Life clubs in the county. The thought of having all that paperwork for just a four-hour event seemed like an unnecessary hassle.

When he handed me a copy of his report in the emergency room lobby, the police officer sighed and shook his head. He didn't have to say any more. I heard him loud and clear. It was time to tighten up the way we ran our ministry events.

Threats to Your Youth Ministry

"Accidents in youth ministry aren't just probable; they're

inevitable," states David Wager, director of Silver Birch Ranch in northern Wisconsin. "Despite our best efforts to prevent them, accidents will happen. The challenge for us is to be trained and prepared to deal with them so we can save a life."

Wager believes that there is a mentality among some religious people that stresses trusting in God and *hoping* accidents won't happen. Consequently, many times religious people are the least prepared to respond to an emergency with practical training and skills.

You Need Professional Help!

Information about legal matters, insurance coverage, and permission forms are extremely important to the solid foundation of your youth ministry. The material in this chapter is neither comprehensive nor intended to be used as the sole counsel for the decisions your youth ministry makes on these important topics.

Each youth minister should find an attorney and an insurance agent who are qualified and knowledgeable in these subjects as they relate to youth ministry. Incorporate these professionals into the decision-making process of your ministry. Use their skill to design operation and insurance coverage policies appropriate to your local community.

In addition to lack of proper training, Wager lists the possibility of sexual abuse by staff, the lack of proper permission and health forms, and the substandard condition of vehicles and drivers used for youth ministry as major threats to the safety and credibility of a youth ministry.

In many cases, safety problems reflect economic struggles. Some Christians are reluctant to pay for what really needs to be done to make their youth ministry safe. They don't think they can afford the time or money to send staff through a certified first aid program, to repair and maintain their vehicles, or to buy the insurance coverage needed to protect the young people under their care.

For example, one small summer camp organization ran a great program for young people every year. The camp leaders provided much of the money for its operation out of their personal finances. When they were faced with the choice between spending $1800 on additional insurance coverage or purchasing new canoes and sports equipment, they opted for the canoes. A year later, after a young man was killed during a camp activity, a lawsuit was brought against the camp and its leaders. They were judged to have been negligent and were ordered to pay damages far beyond the insurance coverage they carried. They lost the camp property, and several leaders had to pay large sums of money out of their own pockets. The ministry of that camp was halted because the leaders unwisely chose not to purchase the additional insurance.

Every day the threat of legal action against churches and youth organizations is increasing. There is a growth in litigation on all fronts as people seek damages from those they accuse of harming them. People are less hesitant to bring lawsuits against churches. In some states, legislatures have removed some of the legal protection that churches and other nonprofit organizations previously enjoyed against lawsuits. Accidents and injuries are inevitable, and so are lawsuits. Youth ministries must be prepared.

Negligence and the Law

Negligence is an unintentional breach of a legal duty causing reasonably foreseeable damage that wouldn't have otherwise happened. In lay terms, a youth leader is responsible to lead the young people under his or her supervision and to make decisions about safety that any reasonable person would make to avoid danger. If someone is injured because the youth leader did not exhibit those safeguards, the leader is negligent and will be held responsible for any mishap.

Legally, the following tests are used to determine if negligence has occurred.

1. A duty: an obligation recognized by the law requiring a person to conform to a certain standard of conduct for the protection of others against unreasonable risks.

2. The act: a failure on the part of such person to conform to the standard required.

3. Proximate cause: a reasonably close causal connection between the conduct (failure to conform to the appropriate standard) and the resulting injury.

4. Damages: actual loss or damage to the interests of another.

All four elements must be proven to establish that a defendant is negligent, thus allowing the injured plaintiff to recover damages. To establish that a defendant is not negligent, one need only show that one of the tests was not met.

The standard of care the law requires is not absolute safety but reasonable actions in view of the probability of injury to others. Whether or not you are negligent depends upon how you acted. The standard of care required is measured by comparing it to what a person of ordinary prudence would exercise under similar circumstances. A reasonably prudent person demonstrates the sensible caution and care the people of a community would expect a normal person to exercise. Negligence is the failure to exercise that degree of care that is reasonable under the circumstances.

An additional important consideration in establishing negligence is foreseeability. If, in the eyes of reasonable people, an occurrence could not have been anticipated, a leader cannot be held responsible for not providing protection against it. Obviously, a leader does not want anyone

Why Parents Sue
■ ■

1. Surprise! The parents had no idea that their kids would be doing the activity in which they were injured.

2. Lack of communication. When the youth leader seems unavailable or uncooperative in providing information about an event or after a young person has been injured, the parents' anger rises.

3. Wrong decisions. If parents feel that a mistake was made by the leaders in planning or allowing a certain activity, they might sue to change the way decisions are made about youth group activities or their supervision.

4. Covering up. When parents feel that an organization is withholding information or trying to transfer blame, they may become angry enough to sue.

5. Young leaders. When young leaders are the primary staff leading an activity during which an accident occurred, parents can jump to the conclusion that their child was not supervised by a capable leader.
■ ■

harmed, even unintentionally. But if the consequences could have been foreseen by a reasonable and prudent person, such a person, it follows, would have taken precautions. The reason for a leader's failure to foresee the consequences—whether carelessness, bad judgment, excitement, inattention, inexperience, ignorance, or forgetfulness—is immaterial, even though the leader was acting in good faith. The "reasonable and prudent professional" must be able to foresee from the circumstances a danger to the participant, a danger that presents an "unreasonable risk of harm" against which the participant must be protected.

A full discussion of liability and negligence is beyond the scope of this book, so you should discuss them in greater detail with a local attorney trained in this area of law. You can obtain additional information from books that address legal liability, negligence, and risk management. For a comprehensive summary of court rulings on lawsuits related to youth activities and recreation, see Betty van der Smissen's *Legal Liability & Risk Management for Public & Private Entities* (3 vols., Anderson Publishing Co., 1990).

You don't have to be a law student to have a basic understanding of negligence and the standards by which you as a youth leader will be judged. The purpose of this book is to motivate you to assess your program to determine if you are inside the boundaries of "reasonable action." To that end, the true stories contained in each chapter will help you develop a higher degree of foreseeability as you plan and lead activities and events.

Insurance Protection

What coverage should a church or youth organization consider?

Commercial general liability. This type of insurance protects you in case of a lawsuit in which negligence is charged. It also provides legal defense to protect the organization and any individuals named in a lawsuit. Whether or not they have strict safety practices, most organizations will be sued at some point in time. In today's legal climate, it is virtually inevitable.

The amount of general liability coverage a church or organization should carry will vary according to several factors, including the size of its operation, the amount of its exposure (the number of activities and students involved), and its geographic location. It is difficult to state a rule of thumb for the amount of coverage needed, but a minimum starting figure is $1 million. Anything less than $1 million is simply not realistic today and would not go very far if, for example, the church van had an accident in which two young people were killed and six others were seriously injured. Insurance agents agree that a church can't buy too much insurance for the coverage of young people and youth activities. Emotions run high and strong when young people are injured or killed. After a tragic accident, everyone wishes he or she had more coverage.

You should make your decision regarding coverage in consultation with a reputable insurance agent. The agent can help your church or organization determine both your potential liability and what kind of premiums you can afford. Today many youth ministry organizations carry coverage between $2 million (with a $5 million excess or umbrella policy) on the low end to $25 million on the high end.

Liability insurance most often pays for the injuries and damages suffered by people we know and care about, not for strangers who are trying to get rich by suing us. Usually our coverage will be used to help the families and kids for whom we conduct youth ministry. If they are seriously injured, why should they be shortchanged by our lack of planning and failure to provide adequate coverage?

A major exclusion on most general liability policies is sexual misconduct by staff (paid and volunteer). This problem is gaining increasing publicity as more and more young people are willing to come forward with charges against adults who have abused them. This is discussed under "Staff Selection and Supervision" in chapter four.

Activities medical insurance. This accident/sickness policy can be purchased to cover medical bills incurred by young people injured during ministry activities. This coverage can pay for the immediate expenses and prevent families from going into litigation to recover medical bills. Since most families have medical insurance coverage, you should note on the parent information and release form that their insurance will be used as the primary coverage in case of an injury. In this case, the youth ministry accident policy will be used as a backup for what a family's primary coverage does not cover.

The youth ministry or church can arrange special event insurance for families who don't have medical insurance. This insurance can be purchased for a nominal fee (one to two dollars per person, per event) for a day, for a weekend, or for youth ministry activities throughout the year. It is best to build the cost of this insurance into the price of the activity. The youth ministry can buy the policy for the entire group. Insurance companies offering this type of coverage want to know the number of young people being covered, not the names of those who want the coverage and those who don't. If someone whose family doesn't have personal medical insurance is injured, the youth ministry pays that person's medical bills and then submits those bills to the insurance company for reimbursement.

Automobile liability. Churches should carry adequate coverage (suggested amount: $500,000) both for vehicles they hire and for vehicles they own. In addition, any drivers who carry passengers should be screened carefully for acceptable motor vehicle records *and* required to carry adequate liability coverage (suggested amount: $100,000/ $300,000) on their personal vehicles. Vehicle safety and insurance are discussed in more detail in chapter five.

Workers' compensation. Workers' compensation requirements vary from state to state, with some states having lower requirements or exemptions for churches than for other businesses. In some states, the number of employees determines an organization's liability to provide workers' compensation. Other states have a statewide fund to cover claims. Although most people are not aware of it, workers' compensation does apply to volunteer workers and paid employees. Volunteer staff who are hurt while on the job (for example, playing basketball at a retreat) might be covered for a work-related injury. Check with a local insurance agent to determine your exposure and responsibility.

Additional insurance. Insurance coverage for watercraft, aircraft, other equipment, and activities excluded from your general liability policy can be obtained on an event-by-event basis if you need it. The cost of the premiums, however, will be significant. Also, coverage for counseling/omissions and errors liability is recommended for professional counselors. Youth workers who counsel informally as part of their other activities are generally protected through their church or organization's general liability policy.

Health and Liability Release Forms

Are those pieces of paper with parents' signatures on them really valuable and necessary, or are they worthless and a waste of time? Most youth workers with a few years of experience have at least one release-form story to tell. Perhaps they took a student to a hospital for treatment, only to be told that the paper was worthless and that the hospital staff needed to talk with the student's parents by phone before they began treatment. But when they visited another hospital some time later, they found a different procedure and attitude.

Health and liability release forms won't solve every problem, but they can be a valuable tool to protect everyone involved. Using them helps you provide the best care for students involved in your youth ministry program. In an emergency, a signed health form might make the difference between a student receiving immediate care or having to wait until a family member can be contacted. Access to a person's complete medical history gives the hospital staff important medical information that may speed their ability to make a correct diagnosis and treatment. Having complete factual information about students, their families, and their insurance helps you complete the extensive information forms used in most hospitals.

You can create your own health and liability release forms. (See the sample form on pp. 225-229 to see what to include.) But make sure you review whatever form you decide to use with a local attorney and with medical personnel from a local hospital. They will help you identify any other information needed in your local situation.

Helpful Tips for Using Health and Release Forms

Every form should be filled out legibly and in ink. Printing is best. Make duplicate copies of all forms and keep a set in your office. A great way to get all the release forms at once is to hold a parents' information meeting prior to a trip or event. Explain the activity or trip to the parents and students. Ask them to complete the forms before they leave the meeting. The meeting can fulfill the multiple purposes of information, registration, and presentation of requirements and rules.

Health forms can be filled out annually (or every six months) and kept on file for students who are active in multiple activities that require a health form. But a parent's signature is required for each activity to confirm that the health information given previously is still current.

Remember that adult staff also need to complete forms. Their medical and family information will be needed if they are injured.

Most important, you must have immediate access to the forms when you need them. Work out a system that allows several people to know where the forms can be found. Keep the forms in a central location that is easily accessible (not locked in a suitcase or the trunk of a car). If your group is traveling in multiple vehicles, distribute the forms for the appropriate students or adults with a leader in each vehicle. Then if you are separated or in an accident, you will have all the appropriate information with you.

After a trip, collect the forms and keep them on file. Consult with a local lawyer about how long you should keep them in your records.

Specific Activities Liability Release Form

While the medical information form can be stored on file and used as long as the medical information is current, the activities release form must be filled out and signed for every specific event. (See the sample form on pp. 228-229.)

The activities release form should describe the event and list the dates for which permission to participate is being given. By signing, the parent or guardian is giving permission for the young person to be involved.

As noted earlier, many youth workers believe that a release form is a worthless piece of paper. Its value and importance continues to be a source of debate. A signed release form does not protect a group or leader from being sued by a parent for negligence. In legal terms, no one can "contract away" negligence. The leader still must act reasonably to provide safety and protection. A signed release does prove, however, that a parent or guardian gave permission for his or her child to attend the event or activity.

An organization can protect itself by listing on its release form the specific activities in which students will participate while they are under the care and supervision of the youth group leader. One of the major causes of lawsuits involving youth programs is surprise. Parents with little or no knowledge of the activities in which their kids were participating are understandably upset when something goes wrong.

You can solve this problem by providing more information to the parents prior to a trip or event. You can verbally explain an activity to the parents at a pre-event meeting, but you should also put that information in writing and give it to the parents. Listing a series of "risky" activities and asking parents to initial their approval of a son or daughter's participation makes a much improved consent form that gives parents prior knowledge.

Listing specific activities on the release form requires the leader to produce a fresh form for each event. You can reduce your work by keeping your basic information on a computer disk or in the form of paste-up art.

For what types of events or activities do you need release forms? A lawyer will tell you to have forms completed as often as possible. The trick is always to have it when you have an accident or incident. Here are my recommendations:

- an overnight trip—always
- a day trip out of your area—always
- any activity out of the ordinary—always
- normal, regular youth activities—get one form signed; keep one copy on file and one copy with you.

Check with a lawyer to work out the wording for the forms he or she recommends. In addition, keep the lines of communication open with the parents of the young people involved in your program. More contact and communication will mean fewer problems and reduce the chance of legal action.

Your commitment to safety and protection will be tested when a student arrives at the departure point for an overnight trip without a signed release (or medical) form. It would be very foolish to allow that person to go on the trip, despite the pressure you will feel from yourself and the other students. Send a message to everyone in your group about keeping the standards. They will thank you several years later for standing firm. Better yet, get parents to sign the forms at your informational meeting. Set an early deadline for paperwork to be completed and for the money to be paid. Don't let everything wait until the last minute.

Protecting Yourself

Establish an oversight group. Whether your ministry is large or small, demand from your church or organization a group of people to whom you will be accountable. The group could be composed of four to ten people who have interest in the youth ministry. A mixture of people by age, background, and occupation will give you a balanced group—and be sure to include some parents.

Discuss your plans for the youth group with this oversight group. Ask them for their feedback and suggestions. They are not meant to determine the strategy or goals of the ministry; they are there to help you find common-sense solutions to the problems you face and to give you honest feedback about the plans you make. Make safety a regular discussion item. Report to this group any accidents or near misses you experience and ask for their advice as you plan future events.

If you discuss safety matters with this group and heed the advice that they offer, you will have a strong defense for the "reasonable and foreseeable" preparations you make to protect the young people attending your program. Meet at least quarterly. Keep notes of all the meetings and file them in a safe place. On some pressurized day in the future, you'll be glad you have verification of your commitment to safety concerns.

Keep written records. It seems that most youth ministry leaders hate pencils and paper. Still, leaders need to get over their fears and laziness about keeping written records. Build files and notebooks of any relevant safety information. Prepare a written report for each accident that happens in your ministry. In counseling matters, keep written records of all conversations with students. Such records will be invaluable if you are ever charged with pastoral or counseling malpractice. Note dates and times as well as any directions or counsel you gave to a young person. These files should be kept under lock and key and must remain confidential.

Because many lawsuits take place several years after the incident occurred, you cannot trust your memory to recall all the necessary facts. Written records are a must.

Remember who your protection really is. It is vital to remember that, while we are called to cooperate and act responsibly in affairs governed by humans, we answer to a higher court and a higher judge. Everything we do and say related to matters of safety should please God and bring glory and honor to the name of Jesus Christ.

The Parents Were Happy
■ ■

We spent our winter break in Asheville, North Carolina, on a work project. In addition to four days devoted to physical labor, we set aside time for extra activities such as rappelling, hiking, climbing, and white-water rafting.

In addition to our usual medical permission and liability forms, I prepared an activities permission sheet that detailed the planned special events. There was a description of each activity and a line for parents to initial their approval or rejection. The pre-approved participation was a change from my usual policy of unmentioned and sometimes spontaneous activities.

The parents loved it. Every fear and concern was addressed before we got into the van. No imaginary unknowns, just clearly defined situations. If a parent had reservations, we were able to talk about them before we left. It avoided the occasional post-trip reaction of hysteria: "You did *what*?" The parents also understood that I had no intention of putting their kids into situations they didn't want them in. I valued their opinions and made safety a priority. All my future retreats and trips will include an activities permission slip with specific details parents can initial.

Michael Collison

New Life Community Church

Sayville, NY
■ ■

FOUR

How Well Do You Know Your Staff?

■ ■

I couldn't figure it out. Carolyn had been one of our strongest student leaders during her junior year in high school. During her senior year, when my hopes and expectations were so high for a great ministry in her school, she practically dropped out of sight. She seldom came to the meetings. Whenever I saw her on the streets or called her on the phone, she always seemed uneasy. For years I struggled with guilt, thinking that we had burned her out the first couple years of high school and contributed to her spiritual crash by keeping her too busy and failing to feed her spiritual life or meet her needs.

Five years later, one of Carolyn's high school friends sat in our living room talking about her new job and reminiscing about her days in the high school ministry. I raised my question about Carolyn's senior year disappearance. Her friend said that Carolyn had had a difficult year because of her agonizing decision to have an abortion. Abortion? I didn't even know she was pregnant. Who was the father? The name struck me like a knife—Tony.

Tony had been one of our youth ministry volunteer leaders during the time Carolyn was in school. He was single, mid-twenties, eager to serve God, and always ready to discuss the Bible. His commitment to the ministry had declined during the year we lost Carolyn. Through it all he had talked a good game and kept me in the dark. That dirty rat! He used his position in the youth ministry to hurt a young woman whom we were supposed to be teaching biblical morality. How could I have been so blind to what he was doing behind my back?

Sexual Misconduct of Staff

One of the most difficult things about being in youth ministry for over twenty years is that I've seen numerous friends, professional ministers, and volunteers violate the sacred trust relationship by drawing teenagers into romantic and sexual relationships. Some of these crimes have been obvious (almost predictable); others have been a complete surprise and a total shock—committed by people I never would have suspected. I have learned from experience how skillful a sex offender can be when he or she is hiding the truth.

Maybe you wonder if this is a safety issue. How can it not be a safety issue when young people are emotionally scarred and physically violated? It certainly is a legal issue and the reason for a growing number of lawsuits against clergy and counselors. Some clergy are presently being charged and tried for incidents that happened many years ago.

Sports teams talk about getting everyone on the same page of the playbook. A successful team is built with people who are qualified to be there, possess a strong desire to reach a common goal, show a willingness to set aside personal desires for the goals of the team, display an openness to instruction by the coach, and will not tolerate anything less than their best effort. Youth ministry requires a similar team attitude and commitment to shared goals. Sadly, many youth ministries drop into losing patterns because people like Tony betray the team goals in their selfish pursuit of personal drives and needs. Other examples abound:

■ One married male youth leader had a real tight bond with all of his junior high boys. He did so many special activities with these boys that the people of the church honored him repeatedly. He was very protective of his group and, citing theological reasons, took a strong stand against cooperative events with other youth groups. A year later the church learned the shocking truth. This model youth leader had numerous homosexual encounters and relationships with the boys in his junior high group.

■ A talented male youth leader, again married, started home Bible studies with a sixteen-year-old girl and her friends (all girls) in her home after school. Within a few weeks, interest in the Bible study waned, but the youth leader continued meeting alone with the girl. The Bible studies included back rub massages, which led to him fondling her regularly. He knew it was wrong and a betrayal of his commitment to his wife, but he couldn't seem to stop. Neither could he tell any of his friends in the ministry or his pastor. Eventually, the girl confessed what was going on to her mother, who reported it to the pastor of the church. When the youth leader was dismissed, the rumor mill worked overtime.

Cry Rape
■ ■

"He tried to rape me in the car on the way here," Denise shouted as she entered the living room. She pointed her finger at Gary, one of our best volunteers. His face turned an ashen white.

"He did not!" countered Jennifer, who was ten steps behind Denise, "I was in the back seat the entire time. He didn't do a thing." Slowly the color came back into Gary's face. Everybody laughed. Denise had made her first joke of the night.

But what would have happened if Jennifer hadn't been in the back seat? Denise loved attention and regularly bent the truth to serve her own purposes. Accused without a witness, Gary might not have stood a chance.

We wised up! None of our male staff drove any females alone to any of our meetings the rest of the year.
■ ■

■ When a sixteen-year-old girl was legally removed from her abusive home, a female youth ministry volunteer, single and in her early thirties, offered to take her into her apartment. At the youth group meetings they seemed like a perfect match, almost inseparable. Later in the year, their participation in the youth ministry declined to sporadic at best. The female volunteer said she was meeting the young girl's spiritual and emotional needs in a personal one-to-one relationship and didn't need to be at the group meetings. Within several weeks, the teenage girl told several of her friends that the volunteer had helped her realize she was a lesbian and that they were sharing that relationship together.

■ A dynamic male youth leader developed a bad habit of focusing on several key students (usually girls) when he was on ministry trips without his wife. He would shower these special girls with extra attention and win their loyalty with long, deep discussions about the hurts of life. The teenage girls loved to sit next to him and lean their heads on his shoulder while he talked about God's love. He knew that one girl was especially open to his leadership because of recent disappointments in her life. She was eager for a change in her life and hoped that his faith would rub off on her. Late one night, after a long one-to-one talk, he attempted to take the relationship to a deeper level by leaning over to kiss her on the lips. When she rejected his advances, he tried to explain away the entire incident as a big misunderstanding. Six months later, when the young woman told a counselor what had happened, it set off an investigation process that cost the youth leader his position in the ministry.

The level of sexual contact and criminal misconduct in these cases, including Tony's, differs, but they are united by a common factor: betrayal of trust. Each of these youth ministry leaders and volunteers crossed the line of moral and ethical behavior that parents expect when they put their children under the supervision and influence of a youth minister. These adults willfully used their positions of influence to gain emotional or physical satisfaction from a young man or woman entrusted to their care. They exposed the vulnerability of the young people, took advantage of it for their selfish reasons, and broke the trust.

When Staff Betray the Trust

The kids are the victims. Physically, the kids may be forced into dealing with pregnancy, abortion, and sexually transmitted diseases. Emotionally, they are scarred by the seduction and betrayal. They are generally dropped from their "special status" with the leader and often feel the ridicule of their peers. Sometimes they are blamed for the dismissal of a popular youth leader. They feel guilt and shame for what they have done and the lies they have been forced to live. Their family relationships become increasingly tense. Spiritually, they lose faith in God and in Christian leaders. They see hypocrisy everywhere and resist trusting any spiritual counselor. Guilt, shame, and depression block their abilities to pray. They often launch out on a self-destructive lifestyle, believing nothing in life really matters. It's crash and burn for them.

Child Abuse

Child abuse is an abuse or misuse of power and authority over a child under the age of eighteen by any adult who is responsible for that child.

Lawsuits and/or criminal prosecution will follow. None of the stories told at the beginning of this chapter provoked a lawsuit or criminal action, probably because they happened several years ago when families were less prone to sue or expose private matters to the public eye. Today many of the taboos about legal action against churches and religious organizations have been removed. Even so, parents are still reluctant to put their teenagers through a public proceeding that would attract media attention. However, there is a dramatic increase of young adults coming forward with allegations of being molested or abused when they were underage. Adult leaders who become sexually involved with children or teenagers can expect to be looking over their shoulders for years to come, waiting for the anger to explode in some type of legal action. The church or youth organization can also anticipate being charged with some type of negligence for allowing an employee or volunteer worker to harm the child.

The bad news spreads. Parents, the media, the community, and students hear the news and judge the ministry accordingly. Good news seems to move like a snail, but bad news travels like wildfire. And the sins of one person can bring down the good reputation of an entire church or youth organization.

The youth ministry atmosphere changes. Staff and young people feel betrayed by the offender. The hypocrisy present in the offender makes people much more skeptical of each other, their faith, and their involvement in the youth ministry. Relationships are strained as people wonder what other secrets have been hidden in the group. People experience a sense of shock and grief similar to the feelings associated with a physical death. Students and adults go through the steps of grief (emotional shock, denial, anger, remorse, grief, and reconciliation) as the news of a leader's misconduct becomes public. Group members find it harder to trust each other because a key link of trust has been betrayed. Drops in enthusiasm and attendance are also common byproducts of a leader's misconduct.

Other Kinds of Misconduct

Not every misconduct involves sex. Sexual misconduct is a major issue because of the powerful forces involved. The appetites and attractions are strong; the consequences are equally rugged. It has been a fatal attraction to many men and women for thousands (Yes, thousands!) of years. Satan has gained mastery over many people by enticing them with sex and power. But other types of misconduct can arise when staff are not properly screened or trained.

Ted came on the retreat as a last minute replacement counselor. Several of the staff leaders knew him as a twenty-seven-year-old, mild-mannered, solid Christian man. He was assigned to a cabin with eight junior high boys, all from difficult family situations.

At 2 a.m., the light was still on in Ted's cabin, and the youth group supervisor thought that the unusual amount of noise coming from the cabin offered a good reason to stick his head in the door for a quick check. When he opened the door he saw Ted looking like a raging bull and holding a twelve-year-old young man in a vicious headlock. The emotional stress of putting eight young teenagers to bed had snapped Ted's patience. He was on the verge of doing something to this boy he would regret the rest of his life.

The youth group supervisor defused the situation and immediately moved another experienced counselor into the cabin with Ted for the rest of the night. When the leader talked about the incident with Ted, he realized that under this mild-mannered veneer was an angry man who snapped under pressure. In the rush to get enough counselors for the weekend, they had screened Ted in ten minutes only three days before they left.

Staff misconduct can also include money mismanagement, drug or alcohol use, racial prejudice, the use of foul and abusive language, lying, gossip, disrespect for authority, and any other sins listed in the Bible. Of course, don't forget the "sin" of disregarding the health and safety of the kids in the youth program.

Everyone in youth ministry will fall short of perfection, but we need to set staff standards of attitude and behavior high because of the important task given to the staff. An effective youth ministry has a shared commitment to excellence and holiness that models the Christian life to watching teenagers. Everyone who joins the team needs to qualify in the necessary skills and lifestyle.

Staff Selection and Supervision

Because a staff leader's mistakes can cause so much emotional and spiritual damage to so many people, it's just common sense to go to great lengths to select the right staff and to eliminate potential violators. In light of what is at stake, every youth ministry should re-examine their process of accepting and employing leaders (both paid and volunteer) to be sure reasonable precautions are taken to screen out potential offenders.

A local church or youth organization needs a written policy statement on child abuse and a working policy on the selection and supervision of staff (paid and volunteer). The policy statement should spell out in clear language what the church believes about the value and care of children and youth, as well as the church's responsibility in this ministry. It should specify the application, screening, and supervision process of the church for everyone involved with children and youth. All existing workers and applicants should be informed of the organizational standards of behavior and be required to sign the statement agreeing to abide by those standards. A public written statement should be made by the leadership of the church declaring their commitment to report to legal authorities any known instances of child abuse. All applicants must be informed of the church's promise to report any instances of child abuse.

No process is foolproof. Legal authorities simply want to know if an organization has taken reasonable and consistent steps to obtain information to help predict any potentially dangerous behavior by an employee or volunteer. How much information should an organization gather about an applicant? Although lawyers argue about the right of a hiring organization to know versus an individual's right to personal privacy, we can set forth some general principles.

A hiring organization needs to take "reasonable action," which means following any leads or concerns a person's initial application might generate. If an applicant says he or she has been convicted of a criminal offense, the reasonable action is to find out the details of that situation. If an applicant denies being convicted of a criminal offense and there is no contradicting evidence that raises suspicion, the process need not go any further. Prediction of an employee's behavior can only be made according to his or her past performance.

Organizations take "consistent action" by establishing a standard investigation for each level of leadership involvement. That standard should be applied equally without discrimination to everyone seeking involvement in the ministry.

Screening Potential Staff (Paid and Volunteer)

I recommend the following steps in recruiting a youth ministry staff.

1. Have the applicant fill out a written application. I will limit comments about the contents of an application to safety-related matters. An application can also request other types of information related to various topics such as interests, spiritual experiences, beliefs, and the like.

I would also recommend that you ask the applicants to give you detailed information about church membership and involvement for the previous five years. Require the names and phone numbers of previous pastors and youth workers who have supervised them. Find out why they left a particular church and check out their reasons with someone from the church.

With regard to safety matters, the application should ask for a person's education and employment history, with phone numbers to confirm such records. Call these contacts and ask questions that will give you insight into the applicant's personality and behavior patterns. Experienced background investigators suggest that you try to get past the personnel office and connect with a specific teacher or supervisor. The latter are often more open to provide details that will be helpful as you make your decision. Any gap in employment or education is cause for asking additional questions about the period of time in question. Ask about the information on the application to assess its truthfulness.

On the application, include at least the following questions:

■ Have you been convicted of a criminal offense? If yes, please explain. Will you give us permission to check your criminal record?

■ Have you been convicted of child abuse or sexual abuse or been involved in any activity related to molesting or abusing youth? If yes, please explain. Can we check your record?

■ What moving violations are on your driving record? Please list and explain. Can we check your record?

Add other pertinent questions about a person's background (drug use, affiliation with questionable groups, and similar questions) as you see fit.

Conclude the application with the following statement for the applicant to sign and date: "I testify that my answers to the above questions are complete and truthful."

This information protects your youth ministry from charges that you knowingly involved someone with a record of negative behavior. Obviously, the applicant can lie. But if you had no reason to suspect the applicant was lying, it will be difficult for a jury to hold you responsible for involving the person in your program. If you suspect that the information is not truthful for any good reason, you are responsible to probe deeper (as a reasonable person would) until you are satisfied that you know the truth.

The process of checking records varies from state to state. In some states it is difficult and expensive to check criminal records. Most of the applicants you encounter will probably not have criminal records. However, when you do find something, the content is usually significant.

Checks on sex or child abusers are regulated by state government. In many states, you can obtain a request form for information on an applicant by calling your state government's Protective Services or Child Protective Services. In these states, you can generally file a request form with an applicant's name and social security number and submit a fee (ten to twenty dollars) to learn information on a person's child or sexual abuse record. Other states (New York is one example) have tougher restrictions on gaining information. Although legislation is pending to open this information, it is restricted at present and can only be obtained by checking through criminal records. Check with your local city or county police department to determine what the procedure is in your area to check on a person's criminal record.

Driving records, the easiest records to obtain, are probably the most relevant to the type of staff recruited into the youth ministry. You can easily make a case for the connection between the way a person handles a motorized vehicle and his or her projected behavior on a youth ministry team. It certainly *is* relevant if you expect the person to drive youth as part of his or her job in the ministry.

Just because you asked permission to check someone's records doesn't mean that you have to check them all (especially criminal). Just asking can cause people to answer more honestly. Some people will withdraw themselves from the application process when you ask for permission to check. Then you don't need to know the details or pursue it any further. You have your answer—they don't belong on the youth ministry team. If you do check records, your policy and practice must be consistently applied to every applicant. You could be charged with a discrimination suit if you treat any one applicant different from another applicant.

2. Require references. Five references are necessary to get a good picture of an applicant: the closest family member, a former pastor, a friend, an employer, and a current pastor.

Design the reference form to meet your specific ministry needs. It helps the person writing a reference to know what job his or her friend is applying for. Give a brief description of your ministry. Ask questions that will provide insight into the applicant's maturity and character. Ask the hard questions directly and without embarrassment. Give people an opportunity to talk with you directly about something they might feel uncomfortable writing. If, after reading a reference, you still have questions, take the initiative to call the reference for clarification or additional information. Don't shortcut the reference process. There may be information from a reference source that you can't get from anyone else and that might be key to really knowing the applicant.

3. Interview the applicant. Ideally, it is best to have two people interview an applicant. At least one interview should be conducted by someone in the leadership of your church or youth ministry who does not know the applicant well. Interviewing someone you know well seldom turns up new information. Conduct a standard interview with all applicants, asking each person a set of predetermined questions.

Find a professional who interviews job applicants and work with this person to determine the information you want to gain from your interviews. Develop questions that will uncover that information. You will want to know applicants' expectations and reasons for being involved, their attitudes toward teenagers, their relational skills, their abilities to handle conflict and crisis, their special abilities, their legal or criminal histories, and their spiritual commitment to Christ. Take notes during the meeting; then fill in your notes more completely after the interview.

4. Make a final decision. Work with a team of people (including leaders in your church or organization) to make a determination on the applicants. Your decision will be more objective if one person handles the written information (application and references) and another person conducts the interview. Neither person should know the applicant well. Then include in the final decision a member of your leadership team who does know the applicant well. Let the three people discuss the person from their particular perspectives.

Don't be in a rush to involve an applicant in your youth program. A self-imposed waiting period for all candidates would be prudent. A waiting period provides time for extended prayer about candidates and time to discover more about a person. Don't give responsibility and privileges with children and youth quickly.

From a safety standpoint, qualifications to be a youth ministry team member should include:
- responsibility,
- decision-making ability,
- good judgment, and
- trustworthiness.

An applicant's qualifications (or lack thereof) will become more readily apparent when they are discussed in a varied group. By using this information and taking time for prayer, the group can make a decision about the applicant's fitness for involvement on the youth ministry team.

It is worthwhile to consider having a professional investigative organization conduct the background checks of youth ministry staff. These organizations will check according to the specifications you request. Then, if you are ever sued for having someone in your youth program who had a negative background, the agency would be liable for whatever damages were awarded. The obligation would be theirs, not yours. They can conduct an investigation in a variety of areas, including credit, criminal record, education, employment, driving record, credentials, and personal references.

No Shortcuts

This process is lengthy, but it protects you in several vital areas. It eliminates people who are only partially committed to ministry, something you would have discovered at some time during the first six months of their service. It also gives you more confidence that the accepted applicant will not hurt the kids you care about so much. The person can still disappoint you, but you will know it was his or her doing, not your carelessness, that hurt the kids. This process will also serve you well if you are called to defend it in a legal proceeding. It will be clear that you took the precautions that a reasonable person would expect.

At first glance, this application system might seem to be more of a deterrent than an incentive to volunteer recruitment. Volunteers are so hard to find that none of us want to place any hindrances in their way. It makes the shortcut route look pretty enticing. I must confess that many times during my ministry in YFC I have taken the shortcut and placed people in the ministry who were safety risks to our most precious commodity—our young people. I've learned the hard way that poor decisions always come back to hurt you.

But holding to high standards for acceptance as a youth ministry team member can produce a positive public relations affect. Parents and people in the community who hear about your stringent volunteer standards will view your youth ministry as responsible and worthy of their trust.

Training Your Ministry Staff

When an accident or an act of misconduct puts the spotlight on your ministry, investigators will check the appropriateness of the staff you have chosen to employ. They will also check the training you provided to your staff members to prepare them to do their jobs. With regard to the safety aspect of your training program, you should consider providing at least the following training.

Orientation session. Volunteers need a two- to ten-hour basic training and orientation to the ministry. They need to know how the organization works and their role in it.

First aid training. A certain number of the staff need to complete a certified first aid training course. The remaining staff can take a simplified version of the first aid course to learn the basics. Enough staff should complete first aid training that every event can have a trained, certified staff person in attendance.

Identifying child and sexual abuse. All staff members need a training class to teach them how to recognize the signs of abuse and how to report it within your organization so that a mandated reporter can inform the proper authorities. Instructors can be found at a local college or within a local child service or protection agency.

Suicide prevention training. Teenage suicide is on the rise, so find a social worker who can help train you and your staff to respond to suicide threats made by teenagers.

Crisis intervention training. If staff members build relationships with kids, they will witness crisis. The crucial part of this training is helping staff members learn how to recognize when they are in a situation in which they are over their heads and how to get professional help.

Pregnancy, drug abuse, and AIDS training. These conditions touch more and more young people every year, so staff members need to be aware of what to do when they encounter them. Some volunteers can pursue additional training to specialize in these social problems.

Activity training. Training also covers the specific activities and events, such as canoeing, biking, or backpacking, sponsored by your youth ministry.

Maintain records of all your staff meetings and training sessions. Keep a file for each staff member, including his or her application, references, any notes from supervision meetings, and a record of the training the staff member has completed.

Staff Behavior Standards

If we ask our staff members to follow a high standard of behavior, we are responsible to provide them with clear and specific guidelines by which they will be judged. They should read and sign this document before they start working in the ministry. All staff members should re-sign this sheet every year to remind them of their commitment. Use the following sample to create a form that fits your situation:

Staff Behavior Standards
Name of staff/volunteer:
Social security number:
This staff behavior standards document is to be read and signed by all staff annually.

1. Any verbal or nonverbal sexual behavior with any student is inappropriate.

2. Dating or going out with any high school student is forbidden.

3. Discretion must be used in dealing with all students, especially regarding physical contact. Innocent behavior can be misinterpreted. A hug around the shoulders is not sexual abuse, but a full body hug, stroking, massaging, or an affectionate kiss raises questions. Any overt display of affection should be made in a public setting in front of

other group members.

4. Sexual gestures or overtures a student makes to a staff member should be reported to the youth leader so that discussion can be held with the student.

5. "Buddy systems" should be used by staff whenever possible, but especially when working with students of the opposite sex.

6. One-to-one counseling with a student should always occur in a public place—never alone in a car or a private place.

7. Driving alone with a student of the opposite sex should be avoided at all times, especially when working with troubled teens.

8. If it is necessary to ride or drive alone with a teen, special care should be taken with a student of the opposite sex.

■ Don't sit close to one another in the car.

■ Do not come into physical contact with each other.

■ Do not stop the car to talk.

■ If you must stop, turn on the inside light of the car.

■ Avoid physical contact (hugs and kisses) when saying goodbye.

■ Be aware of the time you depart and arrive. Mark those times in your diary or record.

9. Romantic or sexual attraction for a student by an adult leader should be brought up and discussed with the ministry team leader for prayer and guidance.

10. All suspicions of child or sexual abuse must be reported to the ministry team leader, who will report it to the mandated reporter in the organization. That person will report it to the abuse hot line.

11. Any knowledge or suspicion of any youth ministry staff having an inappropriate relationship with a student must be reported promptly to the youth ministry leader. If the person in question is the leader, the report should be made to the supervisor of that person.

Have you been involved romantically or sexually with any student in the youth ministry at any time during the past year?

_____ yes _____ no

Do you know of anyone on the youth ministry team who is or has been romantically or sexually involved with any student in the youth ministry?

_____ yes _____ no

Are you now a child abuser or have you ever been convicted of child abuse or sexual abuse?

_____ yes _____ no

If yes, please explain:

I certify that I have read and agree to abide by the standards and that the statements above have been answered truthfully.

Signature _____

Date _____

The Biggest Threat to Safety

■ ■

What's the greatest threat to the safety of kids in our youth ministry: rock climbing? lightning? drunk drivers? flying pencils? tackle football? cage balls? white-water rafting? snakebites? The most dangerous potential threat to hurt a student in your youth ministry is...an adult leader. The people charged with the care of young people will cause more damage and harm to the kids than any natural disaster or sports hazard. A laceration can be stitched; a fracture can be set; but a betrayal of trust or an inappropriate sexual relationship scars a young person for life. Sexual, physical, and verbal abuse by well-intentioned but immature youth ministry staff does deep damage to a young person and often blocks his or her future relationship with God. The quality of the staff on a youth ministry team is the most important safety factor for the protection of the young people involved.

■ ■

Detecting Staff Misconduct

The best method of monitoring staff conduct is regular supervision of all workers who have contact with young people. Actually visiting them on site and watching the interaction is best. At the least, workers need regular appointments with supervisors to discuss not only what is happening with their time in youth ministry but also what is going on in their personal lives.

Most studies indicate that child abusers do not plan to abuse children when they get involved with an organization. They have the best of intentions, but they get carried away in the relationship. A memorable event with a child or young person expands the emotional or physical contact the abuser has with the child and he or she crosses the line into what is inappropriate, immoral or illegal.

A common sign of trouble is an adult who is emotionally immature and not having those emotional needs met in an appropriate relationship. Potential abusers are often not able to express their feelings or relate comfortably with their own age groups. They find it easier to bond with a child or a young adult. Don't overlook these obvious warning signs even when these people are well liked by the young people.

Innocent indiscretions are easy to spot and correct. Serious sexual misconduct violators are much better at disguising their actions and deflecting any inquiry into their behaviors. They work hard to protect their secrets.

Here are a few signs that signal possible trouble:

■ A staff member regularly spends time alone with the same youth group member.

■ There is more physical contact (such as touching or hugging) than is normal.

■ A teenager becomes more and more dependent on one particular staff leader.

■ A youth group member doesn't mix with other staff equally.

- A staff member and a teenager give unusual gifts to each other.
- The two people in question look at each other in a way not typical for staff-teenager relationships.
- The friends of the teenager and the staff say or imply something suspicious about the relationship.
- The staff member's spouse reduces his or her involvement in youth ministry.
- A teenager reduces involvement in regular youth programs but still shows up before and after activities to see a particular staff member.
- A staff member consistently gives rides to the same teenager and resists offers of other staff members to do so.
- A staff member goes to date-type places with a student outside of youth activities.
- A staff member treats one particular teenager to food, tickets, and so on.
- A teenager becomes extremely emotional without any apparent cause.
- The staff member assumes a defensive attitude or questioning of behavior standards when the subject of possible misconduct is raised.
- A staff member openly defies a written standard of behavior and minimizes his or her actions when confronted.

None of these signs should be taken alone as proof of staff-teenager misconduct. These are only signals of what could be going on outside the youth ministry setting. But the more signs present, the stronger the suspicions should be.

Staff members need regular supervision to help them do their jobs in the youth ministry. Utilize a balance of group meetings and individual appointments. Use this time to address any concerns you have about how the staff member is relating (positively or negatively) to any of the youth. Don't be afraid to ask openly if someone is experiencing any attractions for or feelings toward a student.

If staff members are determined to be secretive, they will be. You have given them opportunity to discuss what might eventually disqualify them from ministry. If you suspect possible indiscretions, change a staff member's job and responsibilities to distance him or her from the young person in question.

If the evidence seems to prove misconduct but the person will not acknowledge it, warn of your concern and promise the individual that he or she will be watched closely. You expect that person to live up to the standards of behavior that he or she signed. Remind him or her of the damage this relationship will have on the student, and request that he or she stop any inappropriate action for the sake of the young person. The staff member may become upset and quit the ministry, accusing you of a lack of trust. Such a reaction may provide the best solution to the problem, for this person is probably covering up and deflecting the pressure back on to you. It is also wise to have a staff member of the same gender cautiously and discreetly ask the young person in question to describe his or her relationship with the adult staff member. The young person's responses can provide additional, helpful information.

Take Action Without Delay

Once you have conclusive evidence that the standards have been violated, take prompt action. Arrange a meeting with the governing board or supervisor over your ministry. Don't be afraid to dismiss or reassign the person to a ministry for a different age group. It will send a strong message to the rest of the youth ministry team that you are serious about the standards.

If you find that the person has been behaving immorally, you must alert your organization's governing body and bring the violator under discipline. You need to carefully confront the student involved, using a same-gender staff member to find out what has happened.

At some point, the parents need to be informed of what happened and what has been done to resolve the problem. This is always very messy and demands a great deal of prayer. It's often wise to have the senior leader of your church or organization lead this process of confrontation, repentance, healing, and reconciliation.

If the teenager-staff member relationship has involved criminal activity, such as an adult having sex with a minor, the parents must be informed immediately. If they choose to

---

Are You a Sex Abuser?

Someone reading these words has a secret to hide. Right now or at some time in the past you have been involved in a romantic or sexual relationship with a student in your youth ministry. If it's you—keep reading.

How long can you keep this secret? It's not a question of *if* you are discovered. It's only a matter of *when* someone finds out. Perhaps you feel powerless to change or are terrified of the consequences of telling the truth. You keep hoping that time will pass and all this will just go away.

You won't break the domination of this immoral relationship until you confess your situation to a trusted leader. It's the first step in breaking free. The consequences will be painful initially, but if you wait until you are exposed by someone else, the consequences will be much more severe. Because you didn't come forward, your repentance and remorse will always be questioned. It will be hard for people to trust you again.

Don't keep this a secret. You will never find relief until you go with your trusted confessor to your ministry supervisor. Pray together and ask those advisors to map out plans for you to repair the damage done to others and to restore your integrity.

---

press criminal charges, the church or youth organization should recommend that each party obtain its own attorney and conduct any communication through the attorneys. The organization must maintain a neutral stance and not appear to side with either the violator or the victim. The legal system will deal with this issue. You can deal with the relevant spiritual issues by involving a pastor (working through the attorneys, of course) at an appropriate time. If the news media become interested, appoint a single spokesperson through whom all communication is given. All other staff should be instructed to make no comment on the matter. You should protect the alleged victim *and* the accused from any statements that might injure their reputations. The less said, the better.

Avoiding Future Problems

When Barry got caught messing around with a young girl in his youth group, nobody could believe it. His wife was so gorgeous. Why would a high school girl interest him? Though Barry had been at the church for only fifteen months, the youth ministry was going better than anyone had ever expected. During Barry's dismissal process, someone talked to his former employer at a church halfway across the country. The man from the former church admitted that Barry had been dismissed from that church for the same reason. When asked why he hadn't told the new church, he answered that he wanted to give Barry a fresh start without being hounded by a bad reputation. Besides, no one from the new church had asked.

Perpetrators of sexual misconduct often repeat their mistakes. Unless they have specific accountability to those who know their flaws and are watching them in their new assignments, they will probably return to their old patterns. If someone is dismissed from your ministry, recommend that this person stay out of ministry leadership for an extended period of time until a restoration process has been completed. If this person ignores your counsel and seeks a new assignment, take the initiative to make sure the new employer knows exactly who it is hiring. You won't be popular, but you will be protecting the safety of a teenager in that youth program. Ask the potential new employer what specific precautions it is taking to guard against another violation. When you are hiring, be sure to ask former employers and co-workers direct questions about any past sexual misconduct.

The possibility of misconduct should motivate you to screen and supervise staff members diligently. Though it is time-consuming, it is worth every effort to keep abuse out of your youth ministry. When a staff member betrays a young person's trust, it does enormous damage to people and the ministry and drains emotional energy and enthusiasm from

---

Do You Just Fantasize?

■ ■

Do you ever fantasize about sexual encounters with students in your youth ministry? The talk shows say it's healthy. Jesus says it's just like committing adultery (Matthew 5:28). According to James 1:14-15, it's a step on the road to actually doing it. Fantasizing is a hard habit to break.

The next time you start coddling some sexual thoughts about a young person in your ministry, think about what you will say to that person ten minutes after it's over. What will you say and do when you find out she is pregnant or that she told her best friend about you? Fantasize about how you will feel when your wife or best friend finds out. Picture the scene when you tell your own children. How will it feel to be leading the youth group when you suspect some of it has heard a rumor about you? Fantasize the whole deal. Now that you see the whole picture, how does that little sexual fantasy feel?

■ ■

---

the youth ministry team. Dealing with problems is even more time-consuming than preventing them.

People make the difference. Two chapters of a youth organization with the same standards and training can produce entirely different results. It all depends on the people involved. Any church can have a good or a bad reputation in a community—depending on the quality of the church leaders. Building a good youth ministry team and training them to work together is essential to a safe program.

Common Mistakes in Volunteer Recruitment

1. We avoid recruiting mature volunteers. We overlook people who have years of experience because we think a volunteer has to be young to relate to teenagers.

2. We sign up and employ volunteers too quickly without thorough screening and orientation.

3. We are overloaded with young, single college guys who have a natural sexual attraction to the girls in the group. Most guys mean well but aren't trained by leaders to understand the forces at work or the temptations they will face.

4. We recruit too few women and put them in nonleadership positions. Women tend to be more safety conscious than men and have plenty to offer when events and activities are being planned.

FIVE

Buses, Vans, and Automobiles

■ ■

"I'm going to do it."

"Jerry, you stay right where you are. I warn you—I will not stop this car."

Moments later, the six young people riding in the station wagon behind "Jerry's" car watched in disbelief as Jerry defied his youth leader and crawled slowly out of the rear passenger side window of the moving car. Jerry, seventeen, was known in the youth group for his radical stunts to get attention. The youth leader was tired of Jerry's immature attitude and was determined not to give in to his little self-promoting circus.

With the car barreling down the interstate at sixty-five miles per hour, Jerry crawled onto the car roof and peeked into each window before exiting into the rear gate window of the station wagon. While the students in the car were giving Jerry the cheers he craved, the volunteer leaders driving behind watched the entire performance in shock, waiting for the worst to happen. Eyewitnesses said they saw Jerry lose his grip at least twice and could not explain how he had not been blown off the top of the car.

The volunteer drivers who had witnessed this stunt rushed to the youth leader when they arrived at their retreat location to express their anger and disbelief. The youth leader, who often worried about his reputation as fun-loving, downplayed the incident and said Jerry knew what he was doing. If he had fallen off, it would have been his own fault. It would have served him right. The youth leader was tired of catering to Jerry and was determined not to interrupt the trip by stopping the car to deal with him.

True story! Here's another.

Another youth leader tells of driving in a car caravan on its way back from camp. Suddenly the side door of a minivan opened while they were traveling down the highway. The young man who had been sitting on the floor leaning against the unlocked door fell out onto the highway. Fortunately, the pastor driving behind the minivan saw what happened and was able to stop in time to pick up the boy, who escaped with only minor scrapes and bruises.

Sadly, a group in California didn't escape so easily. A volunteer driving a pickup truck home from a youth event allowed ten students to sit in the bed of the truck. During the trip, he lost control of the truck. It rolled over several times. Miraculously, no one was killed, but all the young people were injured, some severely. The volunteer carried liability insurance of only $25,000 per person and $50,000 per incident. The group for whom he was driving suffered a major financial setback settling all the lawsuits. The pain from that tragic accident will continue to afflict the families of everyone involved for a long time.

Guilty! That's how most of us in youth ministry have to plead when charged with violations of safety involving buses, vans, and automobiles. The stories above are three extreme examples of safety violations, but they reveal the danger involved when you mix young people, vehicles, and leaders who ignore safety issues.

Everyone has his or her own story. While I was interviewing youth workers for this book, the issues of vehicles and safety came up more often than any other subject. Most youth workers admit to overloading vehicles with too many people, breaking the speed limit, not using seat belts, and committing other offenses for which police routinely write tickets. But youth workers are also concerned about the qualifications of the people they ask to drive their kids around and the mechanical condition of most church-owned vehicles.

Transportation is the most easily recognized danger area in youth ministry. The presence of safety violations and shortcomings make the average church and youth ministry organization quite vulnerable to tragic accidents and subsequent charges of negligence.

Time to Get Organized

An increasing number of churches are recognizing the need for a vehicle committee that sets policies and monitors drivers and vehicles. The committee could consist of four to six people, with representation from the pastoral staff, the church governing board, parents of the youth, and the youth ministry staff.

The vehicle committee should meet frequently until it produces a written policy statement. Once it has established the ground rules of operating the vehicles under its care, meetings can be conducted quarterly.

The written policy statement should address who can use church-owned vehicles and for what reason; state the process of identifying qualified drivers; list the responsibilities of a driver before, during, and after a trip; and provide written guidelines for those responsible for maintenance and upkeep of church vehicles. (A sample policy is located in the appendix on pages 231-233.)

You should also establish a separate policy for the ministry's use of "borrowed" vehicles (vehicles owned and operated by parents and volunteers). Every potential driver should have to meet a standard of qualifications so that no young person is ever placed with an unsafe driver.

Who Can Drive?

There are several key qualifications that drivers need to meet.

Acceptable age. The person should be at least twenty-one years old, but check with your local insurance agent to ensure that this is sufficient. Some companies require that drivers be twenty-five.

Driving record. Each driver's record should be checked for traffic violations and accident records. The committee should consult with its insurance company to decide what constitutes a satisfactory record.

Personal insurance coverage. The committee should know how much insurance each driver carries on his or her personal policy. It is wise to set a minimum level of coverage required to be a driver for the youth ministry. A starting point for minimum coverage would be $100,000 per person and $300,000 per incident.

Agreement to safe driving standards. The committee should provide a written statement describing responsible driving. Each driver should read and sign the statement, and the statement should be kept on file by the committee. Any driver reportedly violating the agreed standard must be confronted by the committee.

Helping Drivers Do Their Best

Drivers are special volunteers who deserve quality treatment. Volunteer drivers need the careful support of the youth ministry leader so that they can do their best. Such support will generally include the following:

Written directions and information. Every driver needs written directions (including a map and phone number) to the destination. Provide in the same packet any money needed for gas or tolls and any special instructions about the trip, such as planned stops to eat or use the restrooms.

Adult support. Depending on the length of the trip, drivers may need other qualified adult drivers traveling with them. These drivers can share driving time, handle directions, and deal with any distractions in the vehicle. Requiring leaders to drive home after tiring weekends with little sleep puts the youth in that vehicle at risk. A reasonable alternative is to bring on the trip qualified adults whose main responsibilities are to drive, to serve as support staff, and to stay rested for the trip home. The extra drivers are also insurance in case any leader is unable to drive home because of illness or injury.

Trial run. Make sure every driver has a practice run in the vehicle he or she will drive prior to the actual trip. Driving a van or pulling a trailer is different from driving a passenger car, so give each driver the opportunity to practice tight turns, parking, braking, and backing up until he or she feels comfortable. Pay attention to seat position, checking for any changes needed to operate the accelerator and brake pedals or use the mirrors. The driver needs to feel comfortable and confident to do the best job for your youth program.

Emergency plan. Prior to the trip, discuss with all drivers your plans for communicating with other drivers or handling emergencies. If you are traveling in a caravan, what will your signal be if someone needs to stop immediately or at the next rest area? What should a driver do if he or she becomes separated from the caravan? How will you handle bad weather or driving conditions? After discussing the possible difficulties, the leader and the drivers can spend some time together in prayer asking God to help them as they serve.

Follow the example. The head of staff sets the pace. The volunteer drivers need to see the one who makes the rules living by the same rules. Uniform observance of speed limits, seat belt requirements, and other guidelines is a practical demonstration to the students of you and your drivers' commitment to safety.

Asleep at the Wheel

■ ■

"I can't believe how foolish we were for many years driving all through the night taking kids to camp in Colorado. I know many nights I was half asleep and fighting it as the van filled with sleeping teenagers raced down the road through the darkness. Now that I am a parent, I realize how carelessly we were hauling that precious cargo."

Gary

youth worker from Minnesota

"The youth leader never sleeps. I am tired before the retreat even starts. Then two nights of little sleep followed by the trip home, and I am driving. That can't be safe for my kids. I know how exhausted I am. Next trip I will have special designated drivers."

Mike

youth pastor from New Jersey

"Five years ago I fell asleep driving a jeep full of teenagers home from a snow camp. Fortunately the snow was piled high along the shoulder of the road. When we hit the bank of snow it caught the vehicle and kept us from crashing.

"I was wiped out after two days of skiing and leading the youth program. The students later told me that as I was driving and dozing, they kept asking me if I was OK. I kept telling them I was fine when in reality I could hardly keep my eyes open. I am so grateful to God for sparing me from what could have been an awful tragedy. I don't take chances now."

Clayton

New York pastor

■ ■

Student Drivers

Try to find an insurance agent who would approve of high school students driving for youth group activities. They don't exist. Take the hint. We are foolishly putting ourselves and our youth at great risk when we let a teenager drive.

Most of us have felt the pressure of teenagers who want to drive for us. They play on our emotions (don't we trust them?) and offer to solve our immediate problems (we didn't plan for enough drivers). It is tempting. Having a clearly written policy about qualified drivers takes the pressure off of us. We are protected by the written rules of our church or organization.

How do you handle the student who is insistent on driving? You can't stop this teenager from driving to your events or meetings, but you can (and should discuss) the request to drive with the student's parent(s). If they approve, instruct this student to meet you at your destination, not at your departure point. Also, no students under your supervision should ride with the teenage driver at any time. If he or she is driving friends to the meetings, take the initiative and talk to all the parents involved, informing them of your policy and of their responsibility if they permit their teenagers to ride with the young driver.

Vehicle Safety

Reliable vehicles are equally as important as qualified drivers in the quest for safe transportation. Failure to provide or maintain quality vehicles for transporting young people can be the primary reason for a tragic accident and the basis of a liability judgment against your youth ministry.

One youth pastor in New York is thankful that his church started using the youth ministry vans to help with the nursery and day care during the day. That state requires a vehicle inspection every six months for vans used in nursery school operations. The youth group benefits because now problems and dangerous situations are fixed immediately. The vans have never been in better shape.

Don't wait for your state to enact similar inspection regulations. For the safety of the young people you love, voluntarily submit to a qualified vehicle inspection every six months. Keep good records. It will protect you against accusations of negligence. You will also be alerted to problems with brakes, the exhaust system, the cooling system, as well as other maintenance needs before you are hundreds of miles away from home facing an emergency.

Before every trip (no more than twenty-four hours of departure), every vehicle should go through a "preflight" check. You don't have to be a mechanic to check if you have:

- a current registration and inspection stickers,
- insurance paperwork required to be carried,
- an extra set of keys,
- a flashlight,
- a first aid kit,
- a repair kit (extra oil, wiper fluid, water, basic tools, garbage bags, rags, jumper cables),
- tools to change a tire and an inflated spare tire,
- seat belts in working order,
- functioning lights and signals,
- wiper blades in good condition, and
- a snow brush or ice scraper for winter conditions.

You can also look under the hood to find answers to the following questions:

- Are the belts tight? Are any frayed or brittle? (It's always smart to carry an extra set. You always seem to need them when auto parts stores are closed.)
- Are the oil, transmission, radiator, and brake fluid levels OK?
- Are the battery terminals clean? the wires in good shape?

- Are the hoses in and out of the radiator in good shape?
- Is the air conditioning unit functioning properly?

In addition, check the tires for proper inflation and for any gashes or bubbles. Also, if anyone will be pulling a trailer, check the lights and the tire inflation on the trailer.

A member of the vehicle committee who is solid in basic mechanics can play a crucial role helping you inspect each vehicle before each trip. It will take pressure off the leader's mind to know that each vehicle has been "cleared for takeoff." Prepare a checklist that can be used for each vehicle. The "inspector" can keep a written record of the precautions you have taken to provide safe transportation.

Protecting the Ministry-Owned Vehicle

While every volunteer vehicle should be treated with the highest care, vehicles owned by the church or youth ministry require some special stewardship. When one vehicle is driven by multiple drivers, accurate records are a must. It's simple to produce a short sign-out form to be completed each time the vehicle is used.

When returning a vehicle, the driver should note any problems or trouble he or she had while using the vehicle. Immediate attention can be given to reports of noises in the engine or of body damage. Requiring vehicles to be cleaned inside and outside when they are returned lengthens their service to the ministry. People treat clean vehicles with more care and caution. A dirty, cluttered vehicle triggers an attitude of thoughtless abuse by students and adults.

Everyone signing out the vehicle and driving it on youth ministry activities should read your basic rules of the road and sign his or her name to acknowledge acceptance of those standards. Some standards that you might want to consider include:
- The vehicle should not be overloaded. Have a legal

limit clearly marked on the sign-out sheet. This legal passenger limit is determined by the number of seat belts legally installed in the vehicle.

■ Every person should have a seat (no sitting on the floor or on the laps of other people) and should use a seat belt when the van is in motion. (Some people may feel that using seat belts at all times is annoying, but it is a smart and necessary requirement.)

■ No doors are to be opened when the vehicle is moving. All doors must remain locked. No body parts can protrude out of the windows.

■ No one is to leave the vehicle when it is stopped in

What Am I Doing?
■ ■

"Every Thursday night after gym night at a local school, we would pack all the kids into the church van for the ten-minute ride back to the church. Since we were always hot and sweaty, a special tradition evolved. We drove with the side door open.

"As the attendance grew and the van became more crowded, the brave ones stood in the open doorway with their faces in the wind, like dogs riding with the car windows down. One night I hit the brakes suddenly as we entered the church parking lot to avoid hitting a cat. Three of the young guys were launched right out of the doorway and onto the pavement. They hit, rolled, and popped up laughing. Everyone in the van cheered and laughed.

"Later that night after everyone had gone home, I prayed and thanked God for protecting those three young men. Driving home I asked God to forgive me for being so stupid and to give me the courage to close that side door next week and keep it closed."

Mike

youth pastor from Michigan
■ ■

traffic or at a traffic signal (Chinese fire drills or similar stunts are forbidden).

■ No passenger should hinder or physically distract the driver of the vehicle while it is in motion.

■ When the vehicle stops, no passenger may exit until either the engine is turned off or the driver gives specific verbal permission.

■ Nothing is to be thrown out of the vehicle at any time.

Insurance

Liability insurance is a top concern for any vehicle owned or used by your youth ministry. There is a simple answer to the question of how much insurance you should carry: You can't carry too much! It obviously pays for insurance agents to give such advice, but the increase in costly lawsuits should motivate every youth leader to re-examine his or her coverage.

No one should drive for the youth ministry activities if he or she has only the minimal amounts of liability insurance. In most states, every volunteer should carry at least $100,000/$300,000 liability coverage ($100,000 maximum per person and $300,000 maximum per incident) as well as a $1 million personal liability umbrella policy. (Chapter three contains additional information about insurance.)

Vehicles (especially vans and buses) owned by the church or youth organization require more than $1 million in liability coverage. In the event of an accident involving serious injuries and fatalities, $1 million of coverage will be quickly exhausted. Inadequate insurance coverage can seriously damage the assets of individual volunteers and organizations, who will be targeted by the lawsuits. The tragedy of the accident will be enough trauma without compounding it with financial struggles.

Handling a Breakdown

Breakdowns are a gift from God! Young people learn more about the Christian faith of their leader when the van breaks down on the trip home than they might during all the programs and meetings of the retreat. For every good message we deliver to young people, God gives us opportunities to live out our faith when we are tempted to lose our temper, worry, or curse the lousy bus or van. It's a lesson in real-life faith they will never forget.

Still, after you have thanked God for such a great opportunity to demonstrate the Christian faith, you have to deal with this major inconvenience, which might range from a flat tire to some type of engine trouble. Here is a plan of action to help you respond to any kind of mechanical breakdown:

1. Do your best to park the vehicle in the safest spot you can find away from the flow of traffic. You may be sitting there for a while, so make it the best possible spot you can safely reach.

2. Unless you are faced with some imminent danger such as a fire in the engine or exhaust fumes, keep the students in the vehicle. Be firm. You don't need additional supervision responsibilities at that time.

3. Look for the problem and determine how serious it is. You may want a knowledgeable person riding with you to help you identify the problem. Also, try to determine where you are stopped so that if you call for help you can give your location accurately.

4. Discuss what kind of help you need and think about where you could obtain it. Remain calm and confident that God will help you through this difficult moment.

5. Return to the vehicle and talk with the students. Describe the situation openly and honestly. Pray together for God's protection and help. Ask kids for their best cooperation and support. It may mean remaining in the vehicle while you try to obtain help or vacating the vehicle while you jack it up

to change a tire. If students leave the vehicle, they should move together to a safe place that you designate and stay there. Most important, keep them away from the road.

6. Exercise your best option. This is a time when a cellular phone (borrowed from a friend or church member just for emergency use on this trip) or having a citizens band radio becomes a useful tool. You can also solicit passing cars to see if anyone has a car phone. Use the phone to call the police or any type of road repair and assistance.

Here is where thoughtful preparation pays dividends. The

Our Guardian Angels
■ ■

It was only two hours each way from the church to the water park, but the route took Mark and his vanload of kids through the center of New York City. When he arrived at the water park, he knew something was wrong with the van. The floor felt hot enough to fry an egg on it. Not being a mechanic, Mark couldn't see the problem. Even if he knew what the problem was, he had no money or time to get it fixed. His job was to supervise the kids at the park.

By evening, the busy day had pushed van problems out of his mind. Their trip home came to a halt when smoke started pouring into the cab of the van. Mark pulled over and hustled the kids out of the van and into the street. It was almost midnight, and they were stranded in the South Bronx.

One adult, twelve teenagers, a smoking van, a notorious neighborhood, and no phone in sight. What would you do?

Fortunately, for Mark that night, four members of the Guardian Angels stepped out of the shadows and answered the group's call for help. His next Bible study with the kids was on the topic of answered prayer.

What preparations and precautions should Mark make before his next trip just in case his Guardian Angels aren't around?
■ ■

---

youth leader needs to carry either a road assistance and towing service membership card or a major credit card provided by the church for emergency use. It is also wise to have a vehicle committee member on call at home during your travel time. The member can be praying for you while you travel and also be ready to receive calls for assistance or advice. The member may want to discuss repairs that need to be made or dispatch a backup vehicle to come and pick up the stranded passengers. That person can also activate a phone chain to alert parents of your probable late return. Plan ahead!

Caravaning

This almost universal method of transporting a youth group to a weekend retreat can be a nightmare if you don't prepare drivers in several basic ways.

■ Each driver needs specific written directions and, if needed, a map to your destination. Drivers should be able to tell passengers when you'll make the food and restroom stops.

■ Agree on a distress signal—flashing your headlights twice, for example—that will tell the lead vehicle to stop.

■ Discuss what a driver is to do if the vehicle becomes separated from the group.

■ The driver of the lead vehicle should be thoughtful of the whole caravan when changing lanes, making turns, and going through traffic lights. All cars should use turn signals to alert the caravan to turns and lane changes. Avoid changing lanes excessively.

■ Stress that there is to be no competition or socializing between cars.

Dangerous Situations

Fogged or iced windows. Never drive your vehicles when visibility is poor. Keep front and back windows clear.

You cannot make good decisions if you can't see the traffic coming from all directions. Don't be lazy. Keep the windows clear.

Backing up. Fogged windows and impaired vision can make backing out of a parking space dangerous. If you are not sure what is behind your vehicle, put it in park, and get out to take a look. If you are in a tight squeeze, have a responsible student guide you out.

Braking time and distance. Whenever you are asked to drive an unfamiliar vehicle, take time to get adjusted to its brakes. Remember that a loaded vehicle takes longer to stop than an empty one. Don't tailgate other vehicles—allow plenty of space.

Bad weather conditions. Slow down! Most accidents are caused by excessive speed for the prevailing road conditions.

Fatigue. Driving through the night with one driver is foolish and dangerous. Provide relief. Make sure your drivers get adequate sleep before the trip home. Better yet, have designated drivers who do not wear themselves out participating with the students during the trip.

The Special Challenges of Winter Driving
■ ■

Mention winter driving, and everyone thinks of slippery, icy roads. But the conditions can be just as hazardous when the ice melts if you aren't prepared. Don't forget to bring:

1. Extra windshield-wiper fluid. It will go faster than ever when the snow is melting and the road is wet.

2. Rags or towels to wipe down the headlights. A day of driving in the slush puts a heavy film on the headlights, reducing the power of your beams.

3. Sunglasses. The sun reflecting off the snow can be blinding.
■ ■

Hiring a Professional Bus

Sometimes it is better to leave the driving to someone else. You can take pressure off your staff and keep them focused on the young people and the program by removing them from the responsibilities of transportation.

Don't be shy about checking the safety records and reputation of professional bus companies. Ask the bus company for names of other groups it has serviced. Call those groups for a recommendation.

There are several safety concerns particularly related to using a professional bus company. Your group should appoint

Off to the Races
■ ■

Beware the manhunt! Rich had just squeezed teenager number eight into his compact car. Everyone was so excited. All these people had to be worth at least twelve thousand points. They had five minutes to beat the deadline and return to the church.

Sneakers attached to legs coming from somewhere in the back seat were sticking up in the air on both sides of his head as he wheeled the car around the corner. Everyone was groaning and laughing simultaneously as he hit the accelerator hard.

Suddenly four concrete posts appeared out of the darkness right across the center of the street. Rich slammed on the brakes. The overloaded car skidded on the gravel and stopped just short of a concrete barrier and the embankment it protected. In his excitement Rich had turned one street too soon and almost ran his car full speed into a dead end (literally).

The excitement had impaired Rich's judgment. The rules of the game said to go faster and overload the car to be successful and win the reward. That long skid in the gravel taught Rich to rethink his activities so that he could keep the fun in and the danger out. The manhunt still works without the time pressure and the overcrowding.

■ ■

one staff leader as "bus captain" to serve as liaison with the driver. The bus captain represents your group and is the communication link with the driver throughout the trip.

Ask the professional driver about any safety standards he or she wants enforced during the trip. Most likely the driver will ask people to remain in their seats while the bus is moving. No one can sleep in the overhead storage area or on the floor.

When the bus stops at a rest area, speak to the students before they exit the bus. Set a time to be back on the bus. Warn students about traffic in the parking lot, and caution them about crossing the road to visit a restaurant or store, especially if it is nighttime. Be sure to count and confirm that everyone has returned before giving the driver permission to leave.

Professional bus drivers are known for their driving skills and savvy. Unfortunately, many of them also drive at high rates of speed consistently above the legal limit. If you feel uncomfortable about the speed or any aspect of the driving, do not hesitate to discuss it with the driver. Express your concerns respectfully but firmly.

If someone on the bus becomes ill, inform the driver immediately. The driver can use the bus radio to contact police or an ambulance if needed. The leaders should have the first aid kit available in the bus, along with supplies to clean up any mess. You should always keep the permission and medical forms handy, not packed away in storage under the bus.

When the bus drops your group at your destination, it may be wise to rent a car for the length of your stay. You could use this vehicle during your stay at a camp or resort to carry any student who might need medical attention.

Camps and Retreats

■■■■■■■■■■■■■■■■■■■■■■■

I'll never forget my first day of eighth-grade church camp. Mark, George, and I were the Three Musketeers—primed and ready to run wild and meet girls. By the end of that first day, the three of us had spent most of our time focused on the same female.

She was older and more mature than the other girls at camp. Mark met her during the softball game when a bat thrown thirty feet straight up came down squarely on the top of his head. George met her thirty minutes later, shortly after he crashed into the backstop chasing my errant throw from left field.

Not to be outdone by my buddies, I met her that evening. I walked out of her cottage with a huge red mark on my neck...but it wasn't from passion. I had been running through the darkness, chasing girls between buildings when I was "clotheslined" by a metal stabilizing wire attached to a light pole. Our special lady took good care of us that first day, but we all agreed that the camp nurse was a little too wrinkled for our eighth-grade tastes.

Crazy things always seemed to happen at camp. It was never like being home. It was a new setting, with new people and no parents. The counselors were young, fun-loving, and sometimes wilder than the kids.

Thirteen years later, eighth-graders were chasing me through the darkness of an upstate New York camp. I had a piece of adhesive tape on my forehead, and the kids were determined to take it off. Our nighttime "wear 'em out" game was a creative adaptation of Cops and Robbers. The tape on my forehead meant that I was still alive. When it was ripped off, I was "dead."

Apparently my number was up. Three husky guys wrestled

me to the ground and began pawing at my face. It stopped being fun when their fingernails ripped across my nose and eyes. At that moment I realized there were eight hundred fingers pawing at 160 eyes all across that camp. I thought I had created a wild and crazy camp game designed to let my junior high kids do what they did best—chase each other and tussle with each other. Instead, I might have been the architect of injury and eye damage for one or more of them.

The "camp attitude" had overridden my good sense. It's doubtful I would have run this Cops and Robbers game at a normal youth group activity back home. But I wanted my kids to be excited about being at camp. There isn't anything wrong with wanting students to have great memories of camp. It just seems that the camp atmosphere causes the leader to loosen the safety standards when, in fact, the situation calls for them to be tightened and strengthened.

Think about it. We don't let our young people run unchecked in the dark through the hallways of our church building or outside church property at night. Yet many of us allow it when we are at a camp in an outdoor setting full of surprises and hazards.

For example, Linda organized a late night Hide-and-Seek game for her youth group at last fall's retreat. During the game she got scared watching her crew run through the woods, jump off ledges, and crash into each other. One girl ran into a clothesline (sound familiar?) and ended up on the ground with the wind knocked out of her. Linda tried to calm her kids' reckless approach to the game. Suddenly it wasn't as much fun.

The next morning at breakfast, she saw one of her girls cradling her arm tenderly. An X-ray that afternoon revealed a broken bone. She hadn't said anything last night because she didn't want to spoil all the fun. During the drive home, Linda mentally practiced how she was going to explain to the parents exactly what was going on when the accident occurred.

Camp is different. Things happen there that don't happen at home—adventure, romance, activities, spiritual openness…and accidents. The basic safety risk for camps and retreats is underestimating how different the camp setting is as a potential safety hazard. We arrive at a facility with a relaxed attitude about safety. Many professional camp directors believe the average youth leader doesn't understand that the normal safety policies from home aren't enough when he or she arrives at camp.

Ingredients for Safe Camps and Retreats

The camp director. Safe and successful camps start with a relationship: the youth leader and camp director working together. Some camp directors are actively involved in every aspect of the camp, while others serve only to provide basic maintenance for the buildings. The youth leader needs to visit a camp months in advance and talk with the camp director to establish a working relationship.

We got off to a really bad start with one camp director in New England during a winter retreat. During the first thirty minutes on the grounds, students broke a light and a chair. The camp director became really gruff with us. During supper, one of our staff flicked some chocolate pudding on a student at the table, setting off a minor pudding war. The camp director rushed out of the dishwashing room, grabbed the microphone, and chewed out all our students and staff. He sensed that we weren't going to control our young people, so he stepped in to protect his property. I am embarrassed to confess that the rest of the weekend we allowed staff members to make fun of "Mr. Grumpy" during meetings and joked with the kids about trashing the camp. I found out months later that a good deal of breakage and damage had occurred with other church groups in the weeks prior to our visit. The camp director's concern was completely legitimate.

Are youth leaders and camp directors partners or adversaries? Experienced camp directors often feel pressure when they host youth leaders who are soft on safety issues. Their sense of responsibility compels them to step in and speak up before someone gets injured. Ideally, they can use those moments to educate the group leaders to the risks and dangers they have learned from experience, but they know they run the risk of appearing to be "heavies." Misunderstanding and bad feelings can be avoided by pretrip meetings in which activities and safety standards are discussed in detail.

Through the Eyes of the Camp Director

■ ■

What safety sins do camp directors see when the typical youth group arrives for a weekend retreat?

■ The type of drivers and condition of the vehicles provide major cause for concern.

■ The program and activities have been planned with little regard for safety and little communication with the camp director.

■ The youth leaders are reluctant to spend a little extra money to pay for the additional services of camp staff supervision for the activities.

■ Groups that want to do their own food preparation underestimate the safety risks in the kitchen.

■ Instead of planning the camp experience together and working to protect all the young people, the youth leader and the camp director become adversaries with regard to safety issues.

■ ■

Many camps offer the services of professional staff to supervise and lead the recreation. Camp staff might include lifeguards, watercraft instructors, winter sports supervisors, and registered nurses. Camp directors often don't understand why many youth groups are reluctant to spend a little extra money to hire additional camp staff who could help monitor and supervise activities. For a nominal fee per weekend, experienced camp staff could be added to the team of workers serving and protecting the visiting group. Safe camps and retreats start with a partnership between host and visitor.

The camp facilities. Nothing beats meeting with the director and seeing a camp firsthand. In addition to eyeballing the camp grounds, inquire about the camp's accreditation. The most widely recognized accreditation is with the American Camping Association (ACA). This organization maintains a strict set of safety standards for staffing, buildings, programs, and services for all types of camps, religious and secular alike. A camp accredited by the ACA demonstrates a high commitment to safety and excellence. A Christian camp can also be associated with Christian Camping International, which requires a high standard of excellence. Identifying a camp's accreditation and association membership gives you a strong basis on which to judge its quality.

When you visit a camp, you'll want to investigate the following primary safety issues.

■ Check that the buildings and sleeping quarters are protected with working smoke detectors, recently serviced fire extinguishers, and emergency exits.

■ Walk through the camp and observe electrical wiring, sanitary conditions, storage of hazardous materials, and the natural and man-made hazards on the grounds.

■ Ask about the accident record at the camp during the past year.

■ Inspect the camp's sports equipment and sports facilities to determine how well they are maintained.

■ Ask about the accessibility of medical facilities and services.

■ Ask if any professional staff (registered nurses, lifeguards, water-sport instructors, and the like) are available to you through the camp.

■ Ask about any camp insurance coverage that would apply to you and your group.

The food service. Whether your group contracts to use the camp's food service or elects to provide its own cooks, special attention must be given to food preparation. An accident on the waterfront or the sledding hill is rare and usually affects only one person, but a lapse in kitchen safety standards could cause the entire group to suffer food poisoning. Ask:

■ Does the cook have training and experience in food service for large groups?

■ Are the utensils, equipment, serving dishes, and food contact areas clean and sanitized?

■ Is a dishwasher available to wash at legal standards of 100 degrees Fahrenheit and rinse at 180 F? Are all items allowed to air dry?

■ Are perishable foods refrigerated at temperatures below 45 F when they are not being served?

■ What precautions are taken to prevent salmonella poisoning? (Salmonella bacteria is present in some uncooked eggs and some raw poultry.)

■ Are workers required to wash their hands frequently?

■ Is smoking prohibited in food preparation and service areas? Are sharp knives and slicing machines used only by adults?

Staff training and emergency preparedness. Here's a pop quiz for you and your camp counselors: What is the first rule of emergency response? Do you know it? You can't prepare your leaders for every possible emergency, but they need to know the basics so they can respond to the unexpected.

It was a dark and stormy night. The camp counselors were jolted out of their sleep by a loud crash on the roof of their cabin. The girls in the cabin began screaming and crying. Wind and rain were pounding against the cabin. It was completely dark; apparently the electrical power had been knocked out. What should camp counselors do in such a situation?

The first rule of emergency response is to think before you act. The counselors quieted the girls and conducted a quick roll call to determine if anyone was injured. Everyone was OK, so they gathered the girls together and calmed them. They took control of the group and their emotions.

They calmly talked about what they should do. Because they were safe and not under any threat, they decided to stay put either until help came or daylight allowed them to see and assess the situation. That was a lifesaving decision, because the electrical power lines had fallen onto the porch of their cabin. Anyone stepping out of the cabin in the dark probably would have been electrocuted.

When the storm hit, a camp staff member assigned to emergency response got up to inspect the camp. He saw the electrical lines on the cabin porch, so he returned to the camp's electrical box to shut off the power. He had never shut down the power for the entire camp in that manner, but there was an emergency response notebook that described what he should do.

These cabin counselors' responses were the product of "What if?" training. They hadn't specifically discussed the possibility of a tree knocking power lines onto a cabin, but they knew they should think before they took any action. They made sure everyone was safe and then proceeded slowly and cautiously. Any panic causing someone to run out the front door would have brought tragedy.

"There is no substitute for a trained, mature staff," notes Bob Kobielush, president of Christian Camping International. Weekend counselors from local youth groups need basic "What if?" training.

■ Do they know where the emergency exits are located in case of a fire?

■ Do they have the number of the police or ambulance crew?

■ Can they find a telephone?

■ Do they know to whom they should report any trouble? How can that person be reached?

■ Can they find a first aid kit?

Give camp counselors as much information and training as you can. Talk through a wide variety of possible emergencies until the basics of immediate response are ingrained in your leaders.

Byron Emmert, veteran youth worker from Minnesota, knows the value of having an emergency response team ready and available. Byron wanted to bring a diabetic young man from his YFC club to summer camp. The young man's mother initially opposed the idea because of his condition. However, two weeks before camp, Byron convinced her to train him so he could administer the injections if necessary.

The first day of camp Byron completely forgot to ask the young man if he had taken his morning injection until bedtime, when the second injection was scheduled. The young man told Byron he had forgotten in the morning, so he had given himself an injection just before supper, at 4:30. He assured Byron everything would be all right.

In the middle of the night, Byron woke to the sound of the young man struggling to breath. He jumped to his aid and found him having some type of seizure. The young man had turned blue.

Byron struggled to open the boy's mouth, ignoring the pain as the teeth bit down on his fingers. He pulled the tongue out of the young man's throat and thrust the bill of a baseball cap into his mouth to act as a tongue depressor. Throughout these stressful minutes, Byron roused the entire cabin of guys and gave directions to find the camp director and nurse.

Minutes later the camp director and nurse burst through

the door, took over the rescue effort, and stabilized the young man. Byron stepped aside with a huge feeling of relief. He took one look at the blood dripping from the deep bites on his fingers and immediately fainted. (At the time, Byron did not realize that he should not have placed anything in the young man's mouth, especially his fingers! A person suffering from a seizure should be placed on his or her side and kept calm and comfortable.)

Was it worth the effort to bring a diabetic student to camp? Byron thinks so. However, next time he will post a sign to remind himself and the young man to stay on the injection schedule. Staff need to monitor young people with similar health needs. Students shouldn't be trusted to remember. Byron now realizes that when he knew this young man was off-schedule, he should have obtained help from the camp nurse before they went to sleep. Most of all, Byron was glad a professional nurse was available to help immediately. He might not have had much more time to save the boy's life.

All staff and leaders need an emergency procedure briefing prior to the camp or retreat. Rehearse the basic safety procedures and the emergency response. The leader can select possible events and quiz each person on how to respond. Written instructions and information on securing medical help should also be provided.

Dangerous Camp Games and Situations

Mudsliding and assorted variations. One camp counselor told me just last week how his group rescued its week of rain at camp by having a mudsliding event. Evidently he and many others are still unaware that some of the most tragic accidents and costly lawsuits involve mud events.

In a well-publicized case several years ago, a youth organization created a mudsliding pit. One student ran, slid across the mud, and crashed headfirst into the hardened earth at the end of the pit. The impact broke his neck and paralyzed him. After that incident, most youth organizations banned activities involving mud. Many insurance companies handling camp and youth activities specifically exclude it from coverage.

The safety principles involved here apply to other games:

■ Avoid games that might result in headfirst collisions with other people or natural objects. The risk of a broken neck and paralysis is enormous.

■ Avoid games that incite reckless or overaggressive behavior.

■ Avoid games that are hard to supervise. If you can't stop an activity quickly, you don't have enough control.

Cage ball (earth ball). This large inflatable canvas ball is used for push-ball type games. Injuries are the result of students being hit full force by the ball. A dangerous way to start the game is to have students from each team run from their end lines to the ball in the middle of the field. The first team to reach the ball propels it forward into the approaching opponent. The results could be shown on a football highlights film. Someone on the second team is often knocked off his or her feet by the oncoming ball. It makes for great video, but the risk to the person absorbing the blow is unacceptable. Ban the running start. Also, remember that the six-foot ball is more dangerous than the four-foot ball.

Students are also hurt when the crowds surrounding the ball are pushing to move the ball. It's a reverse Tug of War, with the forces pushing toward each other instead of pulling away. Anyone who falls can be trampled by the onrushing mob.

The greatest danger using the cage ball is having anyone crawl on top of the ball during the game. This person can easily fall headfirst to the ground and suffer head or neck injuries. One youth ministry volunteer was paralyzed

On the Witness Stand: The Case of Creative Camp Craziness
■ ■

It was a tradition. Every year the youth ministry staff introduced some wild new activity during camp week. The goal was to do something even crazier than the year before.

This year the staff found some old motorless go-cart frames. The campground was situated on the side of a steep hill. They decided they would offer "The Great Camp Derby" by racing the go-carts down the path past all the cabins. With no brakes on these go-carts, the staff decided they would stand at the bottom of the hill, holding mattresses from the cabin bunks to catch the racers as they sped across the finish line. Twenty feet beyond where they stood was a public highway, which was the main entrance to that portion of the camp.

The go-carts rolled during the afternoons of camp. No one got anything worse than scrapes and bruises. Since no one got hurt, how could there possibly be a problem?

Imagine yourself in the courtroom answering the questions of an attorney. For what purpose did you undertake this activity? Why didn't the go-carts have any brakes? Why did you not take any precautions for a car passing by on the road when you held these races? What reasonable safety precautions should a parent expect a youth ministry leader to take to protect the children?
■ ■

by falling off a six-foot cage ball. The ball was sitting on the side of the field after it had been used in a game. The volunteer attempted to climb on top on the ball so he could walk on top of the ball while rolling it down the field. He lost his balance and fell headfirst to the ground. His neck was broken instantly.

Use of the cage ball requires careful supervision. Most accidents with sports equipment happen on the sidelines away from leaders' attention. In this case, the cage ball should have been guarded by a staff leader with strict orders not to let anyone mess with it. It should be deflated immediately or put away under lock and key.

Cage balls can still be used under controlled circumstances, if you follow the following guidelines:

- No running starts.
- Fewer people on a team so the ball keeps moving.
- To reduce the impact of the ball hitting a person, don't inflate it fully.
- Don't tolerate anyone jumping or climbing on the ball.

Pile-on games. Once, at one of my very first youth retreats, two hundred kids were packed into a long, narrow meeting room. The retreat leader, wanting to mix the crowd and get everyone excited, drew an imaginary line down the center of the room and told kids to change sides as quickly as possible at the count of three. Doesn't that sound like great fun? A minute later, the middle of the room looked like a Dallas Cowboys goal line. It took ten minutes to unpile everyone. The innocent victims were the small young boys and girls who were pushed down and trampled by the bigger guys coming from the sides of the room. Three kids were taken to the hospital for X-rays. Five or six more were panic-stricken because they had been unable to breathe at the bottom of the pile. What a "great" way to start a weekend retreat.

Sports games. Most camp and retreat injuries are connected to playing some type of sports. Many injuries are unavoidable (once you make the decision to include sports in your schedule) and common. The major risks involve injuries to the head, the neck, and the eyes. Insurance companies warn against games in which dangerous objects are thrown or launched toward another person. Oversized slingshots used to launch water balloons, paint balls, or flour balls are usually excluded from coverage because of the potential to injure a person's eyes.

If you decide to include sports at a retreat, minimize your risk by following these guidelines:

■ Don't play on any athletic field without first inspecting it for hazards and dangerous debris.

■ Don't use games that encourage any throwing of objects toward another person's face.

■ Don't mix big and small, weak and strong kids in contact sports. Smaller kids usually get crunched.

■ Don't make everyone in your group play the game. The reluctant participant is often the first one injured.

■ Don't incite or encourage aggressive or rough play.

■ Don't let athletic equipment be used without supervision.

■ Don't hesitate to step in and stop a situation that is getting too rowdy, rough, or uncontrolled.

Adhering to these rules would have helped me avoid a situation that almost turned into an ugly scene. At a summer youth conference, groups were encouraged to enter athletic teams in various sports for competition during the week. The boys basketball division was really lopsided. Most teams were weak and unskilled, but two teams were loaded with varsity athletes.

Instead of running the tournament as usual, with all the teams playing each other, I joined other leaders in suggesting that the two top teams play their own best-of-five series for the championship. What seemed like a great idea on Monday had us practically calling the National Guard on Friday. We encouraged competition between these teams from two different cities and backgrounds. Every day the games got more intense. The level of the players was far above the skill of the referees to control the game by making good calls. When the gun sounded to end game five, players were ready to fight. It took a long time to cool down the players. We had encouraged too much competition and allowed it to get out of control.

Good supervision of sports activities means watching to see if anyone is becoming angry and looking to take revenge for any perceived wrong. Be assertive and pull that person out of the game until he or she cools down. The gung-ho teenager who is going crazy swinging his pillow in the giant pillow fight needs to feel the hand of a staff member on his shoulder, warning him to ease up or to sit out.

Hide-and-Seek (and all variations of nighttime madness)

After sports, the second major setting for injuries at camps and retreats is the late night "run wild" games. For example, one youth leader gathered his group for late night Hide-and-Seek. Among the rules: Don't climb any trees. Of course, the youth leader climbed a tree to hide, fell out, and broke both arms. (Do you doubt that there is a God?) Amazingly, this youth leader is now suing the church for damages. Young people love these games, but we must think through the risks they present and design a safety system to keep kids from hurting themselves.

Twist and Run. This favorite camp game (put your forehead on a bat, spin around ten times, and try to run back to your team) is a prime example of how to modify a game to be both fun and safe. I usually enjoy belly laughs watching players trying so hard to run straight and ending up on the ground. It has always seemed like a relatively safe and harmless game to me. During the interviews for this book, however, several youth leaders told me of injuries that took place during this game. One girl fell as she was running back to her team. Her head found the only rock on the entire field. Several more were injured when they crashed into other runners. The chance of injury might seem remote, but the family of the young person who is hurt might not understand those odds.

Maybe you're wondering: Should I stop using this game because I know of several injuries it has caused? I don't believe you have to zap these games because of a few injuries. They are still usable—if you take some extra safety precautions. A creative solution for the Twist and Run game is to assign leaders to run alongside the students and act as spotters, ready to catch them or break their fall.

Double Dare. This popular television show has taken many of the traditional youth ministry game ideas and used them successfully—and safely. These games involve relays and stunts, with plenty of messy goop. Notice, however, the goggles over the eyes, the helmets on the heads, the padding on the elbows and knees, and the spotters throughout the course. Youth ministry can still use these types of games at camps and retreats if we are willing to go the extra mile to protect the participants.

Careful game management means placing numerous trained staff members in position as spotters. Provide a means of signaling any dangerous activities or the need to stop play immediately. Equip the spotters with whistles and an emergency signal. When they sound the signal, a main safety supervisor can sound a portable air horn. At the sound of the air horn, everyone knows to stop and kneel down immediately. With proper preparation and controls, youth ministries can still use these games and activities safely.

Carefully supervise all sports equipment before and after its use. Assign staff leaders to put away all equipment immediately after it is used. Require the use of appropriate safety gear. Jazz up the gear so that it will be fun to wear.

Going the extra mile includes having trained medical personnel (paramedics) on site throughout the games and activities. Youth for Christ and a group of churches in Florida once sponsored a big day of field events. It almost became a tragedy during the first hour when a young man experienced a severe asthma attack. Staff members later admitted that they weren't sure what to do to help that young man. It wasn't a problem because the YFC leader had secured two paramedics from a nearby navy base to be at the event. They moved in with their equipment and restored the young man's breathing.

Whenever I walk into a camp director's office at the beginning of a week of camp or a weekend retreat, I look at the phone and pray I won't have to use it to call some mom or dad with bad news. With good safety preparation and enforcement, your camps and retreats can be positive lifetime memories for your students.

Hotels and Resorts

It's a growing trend for youth groups to attend large conferences at hotels and special resort areas. The rustic, remote campground is being replaced by hotel chains. While there is room for debate about the merits of using a hotel over a camp, the hotel definitely raises some unique safety issues.

The hotel setting. Most hotels are multistory buildings in highly populated areas. If the hotel includes balconies and high overlooks, you must prepare for some young person dangerously leaning over the railing or sitting on it like a bird on a perch. If the windows open, kids will be tempted to hang out them or drop objects to the ground. Strict warnings and attentive staff supervision are absolutely necessary.

Swimming pools, hot tubs, and saunas are an attractive part of the hotel experience. The swimming pools, which tend to be small, are usually overcrowded during a youth conference. Is either a hotel employee or a certified conference staff member acting as lifeguard and enforcing safety standards? Are students following the written rules posted near the saunas and hot tubs? Are the hot tubs regularly cleaned and properly maintained? A buildup of bacteria in the water can cause illness among bathers. If the hotel is usually not busy on weekends, its normal maintenance schedule may not be adequate for your weekend invasion.

Although a hotel's rooming accommodations are generally much nicer than those found in a camp setting, the small rooms (usually four per room) and the locked doors present supervision problems. Students have much more privacy, and it is harder for staff to just "walk in" and discover any inappropriate behavior. Guys and girls have a greater opportunity for romantic rendezvous undetected by staff. Instruction concerning and enforcement of rules prohibiting coed gatherings in bedrooms is an absolute necessity. Staff must be diligent about guy-girl encounters in private rooms.

The privacy of the rooms and the ready access to public shopping areas also increases the possibility of contraband such as alcohol and drugs being present at the conference. Students looking for trouble have an uncanny knack of finding the wrong people. Rules need to be clear and tough. Staff must be polite but tenacious about such destructive substances.

A clear policy about leaving the hotel property must be conveyed to all students and staff. No one should walk or sightsee alone. Staff members should either be with every group of young people or should know where they will be and when they will return. The amount of staff supervision needed will vary according to the setting or the reputation of the area, but staff need to know the rules and enforce them strictly.

Using a hotel or resort moves the camp retreat from a remote, protected location into the mainstream of humanity. The normal operations of the hotel and the area will continue throughout your conference experience, so the leader needs to prepare for possible intruders who could harm the young people.

Once our group stayed at a hotel in Florida for a winter break conference. One sixteen-year-old girl asked to be excused from the evening session in the conference room to return to her room for some headache medicine. We granted permission and posted a staff member to watch her walk across the courtyard to her room. When she arrived at her room, she turned to see three men, twenty-five to thirty years old following close behind her. They had just come out of the hotel bar and were looking for some action. They tried to talk her into allowing them into her room. When she refused, one man grabbed her and pushed himself up against her. She screamed, and the staff leader on watch came running. The police were called, and they escorted the men off the property, warning them not to return. The young woman, however, felt fear and anxiety throughout the rest of the week.

On another occasion, at a winter conference in a downtown hotel, a middle-aged man stepped onto an elevator filled with fourteen-year-old girls. As the elevator moved from floor to floor, he tried to start conversations with the girls. They did their best to ignore him and exited at their floors. Finally, one girl was left in the elevator alone with this man. The doors closed before she realized the danger of her situation. The middle-aged man approached her and began to touch her inappropriately. When the door opened, she jumped out and ran for her room. Her youth leader met her in the hall and joined her in searching for hotel security guards. In the process, they spotted the offender, who responded by heading for the main door of the hotel. They followed in hot pursuit, finally finding a security guard as they reached the door. The offender was disappearing into the parking lot. Security guards searched the parking areas and issued a warning and a description to all the hotel personnel.

In both instances, the girls' parents were called immediately and informed of the situation. They were given complete information and consulted for what they wanted to be done. Counseling and a special staff escort was given to the girls until they felt more relaxed and secure.

Other intruders are less hostile, but still dangerous. The

young men of the towns we visit always seem to find our group and our girls. Some of it is innocent—a casual conversation on the beach or in a store prompts them to visit the girls in the evening. Usually, they arrive with several male buddies to check us out. We are very upfront with our visitors. They are welcomed into the meeting or activities, but we have staff eyes on them throughout their visits. We tell them the ground rules the girls are required to follow, including the rule that no one from the group is allowed to leave the property with them.

Our girls get similar straightforward reminders from staff about leaving the grounds, obeying the rules, and continuing to be involved in the required activities. We try to keep our conversations with the visitors upbeat and positive. This is a great opportunity for staff to talk about the purpose of the group and of our faith in Jesus Christ. Sometimes it generates genuine interest. Others are driven away by it. Apparently, sharing one's faith in Jesus can also be effective as a security technique.

At no time should a student ever get into a vehicle with someone he or she just met. Anything this new "friend" offers to get for the student can be provided by a staff member. Never underestimate the risk of an attack on our young people by a stranger.

Staffing and Supervision at Hotels and Resorts

More staff per students. It is worth the extra cost to provide one staff member for every three or four students at a hotel or resort setting. You can negotiate with the hotel to put one staff in every room of four students by using a rollaway bed or putting a sleeping bag on the floor. With some kids, it is wise to lock the windows and to put the staff on the floor in front of the door at night. The ratio could be one to seven—if the hotel provides adjoining rooms (and

the door is left open) or if trusted student leaders are assigned to each room. When two or more junior high students are assigned to a room, an adult should always be
rooming with them.

Staff-student assignments. Assign staff members to supervise their sleep groups throughout the entire trip. They
should check the attendance of their students at every meeting and meal. If someone is missing, the staff member responsible should take action to find that person and get him
or her back. The same procedure works for activities and
for curfews. The staff members are to spend their time mix-
ing normally and naturally with their students (not the other
adults) throughout the conference or retreat and share activities with them. This not only provides relational evangelism
and discipleship but also puts staff in situations where safety
can be enforced quietly and effectively.

Security. Staff need written instructions about who to
call (with phone numbers) in case of emergency situations.
Every room should be checked by a staff supervisor shortly
after curfew to verify that all the kids are in their assigned
rooms. If anyone is missing, the supervising staff should follow a predetermined course of action. During the day, students should be accounted for and under someone's supervision at all times. During our week-long trips to Florida,
some students have asked to stay at the hotel during the
day rather than go to the beach. We allowed this, but we
also assigned staff to stay with the students and left a written list with kids' names and room numbers. Staff members
kept contact with the kids during the day and watched for
any violation of our rules.

Staff team spirit. Although everyone is assigned to certain groups of kids, every staff member must be willing to
approach any student who needs supervision. If a student is
standing on a balcony ledge or throwing ice in the hall, the
staff leader present is to step in even if he or she doesn't

Open That Door Right Now!
■ ■ ■ ■ ■ ■ ■ ■ ■ ■ ■ ■ ■ ■ ■ ■ ■ ■ ■ ■

We had rented three floors of a Niagara Falls hotel for our winter holiday teen conference. Late at night the staff would patrol the halls to keep the noise down and make sure guys and girls weren't sneaking into the same room.

The noise from one room in the middle of the hall sounded alarming. There was some kind of intense male-female bonding going on behind that door. The female staff called for a male counselor to help her get this door open. Scanning the room assignments list she pounded on the door shouting, "Open this door right now!"

The noise stopped. The door slowly opened. There stood a huge man in his underwear. His new bride peeked out from around the bedroom wall. The hotel had sold one room of this floor to this honeymoon couple. The counselors were speechless for a moment. Finally they said, "Sorry, just doing our job. You see we thought...oh, never mind. Congratulations and good night!"

■ ■

know that particular young person. Any correction must be done respectfully and privately; yelling or sarcasm are not necessary. Young people will respect any adult who approaches them personally (my name is...what's yours?) and rationally (here's why we don't want you doing that).

Staying in touch. If your group is at a large conference at which students have many options for eating out and entertainment, it is wise to establish a group check-in time once or twice a day, during which time every student and staff member should report to a leader individually or as a group. You don't want to go through the whole day not seeing students or knowing where they are. More contact usually means fewer surprises and problems.

Workcamps

Most of the young people raised in Christian families don't need more information; they need application. The workcamp has become a popular site for bringing a youth group alive in its faith. One of the best, and certainly the largest national workcamp organization is run by Group Publishing, Inc. For more information you can call them at 1-800-635-0404. Taking young people to work in various national and international settings generates special safety issues.

Preparation. These trips should not be led by amateur leaders. Find a reputable organization with a track record for successful workcamp projects; then link your efforts to its leadership. Let the experienced professionals do the setup work. Any project that *you* decide to undertake requires a pretrip inspection to determine what is needed. If your group is traveling to a non-English speaking location, find reliable translators to travel with you.

Student preparation requirements include applications, release forms, and health forms—all signed by parents and notarized. If the project is outside the United States or Canada, requirements will include health exams, vaccinations, and signed consent forms for international travel. If students are going to do carpentry work or painting, it would be helpful for them to be trained in those skills prior to the trip. Training should be mandatory for anyone using machines or power tools.

Parents need clear and specific information about the type of work their kids are going to do on the project. This information should be written on the consent form they sign. Parents don't like to be surprised. One church group found the young people bragging (and the parents cringing) at the description of the group repairing the roofs of houses in a poor neighborhood. Parents complained that their young people had no experience performing that kind of work and should not have been on the roofs without prior safety training. The kids had a great time, but the parents were probably right.

Staying healthy. Work teams need to take special precautions to stay healthy at work sites, both nationally and internationally. Here are some tips groups have learned during their travels.

■ Bring plenty of sunscreen and a hat. Sunburn can incapacitate a person for several days. Take caution. The purpose of the trip is to help others, not sunbathe. Do not work without a shirt or in a skimpy top. Any trip that takes you farther south than where you live puts you in hotter sun than you are used to feeling. Drink plenty of fluids, especially when working in hot, sunny weather.

■ In foreign countries, do not swim in fresh water without first asking someone knowledgeable about the area. In some areas of the world, there are parasites that enter your body through the skin.

■ Do not walk around in bare feet at any time. Boots should be worn at all times. Give special attention to lacing and tying your boots. If you need to dig in the dirt with your hands, wear gloves. Hookworm (a type of parasite) enters the body through the skin. In addition, dirt under your fingernails can enter your system through your mouth. Dress like workers, not like sunbathers. Be sensitive to the customs and the dress standards of the country in which you are working.

■ In foreign countries, do not eat any fruits or vegetables that you cannot boil or peel (such as bananas and oranges). Do not eat anything without washing it and peeling it.

■ Always ask your host about the source and the condition of the water. If the water is bad, you do not use it even to brush your teeth or as ice in your drinks.

■ Expect to get diarrhea. Even the slight changes you experience when traveling to other parts of the United States or Canada can cause intestinal disturbances. Control diarrhea with Kaopectate, Parapectolin (prescription needed), or Lomotil (prescription needed).

■ Require every team member to receive an updated tetanus shot. Other shots that may be required for entrance to foreign countries are typhoid, typhus, cholera, yellow fever, and gamma globulin (to prevent hepatitis). Antimalarial pills may also be required.

■ If you have allergies or any other medical condition, bring the medication you will need.

■ Be careful in tropical environments. Never antagonize animals or insects that could harm you. Tarantulas and scorpions are not usually deadly, but they can seriously hurt a person. Black widow spiders, fire ants, and killer bees are very dangerous. Treat them with respect.

■ Immediately treat any broken skin or laceration. Infection spreads much more quickly in tropical environments.

■ Eat light to moderate amounts when eating a native meal in another country. Don't eat new types of food excessively.

■ Many travelers eat yogurt with an active culture every day for two weeks prior to an overseas trip. This can prepare your digestive track for the different foods you will eat during the trip.

■ If anyone becomes sick, separate that person from the group for at least twenty-four hours. Place this person in a special "sick" room. Only the staff leader should be allowed to visit him or her to bring food, medicine, and other supplies. If the person is truly sick, the isolation will protect the team and provide the individual with privacy and quiet for sleep. If the person is just complaining to get out of work, twenty-four hours in isolation will probably prove an effective "cure" and discourage whining and complaining.

Equipment and training. Many groups require power tools to be used only by adults. Students should never use power tools without proper training in safety. They must show knowledge of safety and demonstrate good safety practices. The use of power tools should always require eye protection and the supervision of a trained adult leader. Remember: Parents need prior knowledge of these activities.

Cultural awareness. Two girls on a recent work trip to Jamaica ignored the warning of their leader and broke the no smoking rule. When they disappeared from the group to light up a cigarette, they accidentally stumbled into a police drug trap. They had picked up a pack of cigarettes off the ground, but the pack contained marijuana joints. The girls were immediately apprehended by the local police. It took hours for the group leaders to get the girls released. If you are in a foreign country, stay with a national guide and leader who knows the language and the customs. Listen and learn.

Dealing with accidents. Anticipate accidents and prevent them before they happen. Young people will take chances. It's their nature. They often don't think ahead and look for danger. Lacking experience, they put themselves in dangerous positions. A leader must be there to correct and protect these eager young people.

When a young person is injured or becomes ill, the wise leader will make the maximum effort to seek treatment. On a trip to the Caribbean, a young lady complained of stomach pains. A trip to the hospital brought a diagnosis of appendicitis. The leader spent much time on the phone with her parents, sharing all information so they could make their decision. The group had brought a nurse with them (always a smart idea), who helped interpret what the doctors were recommending. The young girl was flown back to the United States for further examination before proceeding with the operation. That was what the parents wanted. The crisis was handled intelligently and carefully.

Here is another example. A young man was struck in the eye with a piece of sheet metal during a Hurricane Andrew cleanup trip to south Florida. The staff took him to the hospital for immediate help and continued to check on him every few hours when they arrived back at camp. The student told the staff that everything was fine. At the same time, however, he was telling his mother a different story about the condition of his eye. When the alarmed mother contacted the staff and demanded action, the staff leaders did not respond defensively or in anger. They did what the mother six hundred miles away wanted done. Smart move.

What overnight trips are you planning for your youth group this year? Whatever your destination or the amount of comfort your accommodations will provide, the key to a safe trip is advance planning, effective training of staff, and immediate response to problems. Devote significant time to discussing and preparing for safety concerns. The motto of experienced camp leaders stresses a wise commitment to thorough preparation: "You get what you inspect, not what you expect."

SEVEN

Summer and Winter Water Sports

■■■■■■■■■■■■■■■■■■■■■■■■

Summer Water Sports

All week we had played that Beach Boys music really loud at our winter camp meetings on the east coast of Florida. Unfortunately, the water had been absolutely calm for three days. The surfboards and Boogie boards we brought from New York had not ridden a single wave.

The last day we would be at the beach, the wind shifted around to the east and blew in a storm off the ocean. While most of the kids scattered for shelter from the rain and wind, our surfer wannabes ran right past the lifeguard, straight into the ocean now churning with eight- to ten-foot waves.

Within minutes, kids were getting tossed in every direction by the waves. They ignored the lifeguard's whistle signaling them to get out of the water. Our staff had a strange mixture of reactions. Yes, it was dangerous, but this was the kids' last day to have the kind of ocean fun we had promised them. If they were crazy enough to be in the water in the middle of a storm, how could we stop them?

When the storm subsided, we hadn't lost anyone—fortunately. A few guys had "raspberry scrapes" on their backs and shoulders from being slammed into the sand by powerful waves. Others told about how scared they had been when the waves were turning them like clothes in a dryer. As we stood silently and watched our students surf through the storm, we wondered if we should have stepped in and ordered them out of the water.

Water Safety

Is water recreation a real danger or merely a perceived risk? According to the National Safety Council, about six thousand Americans drown every year. Only motor vehicle accidents and falls cause more accidental deaths. Drownings are the result of boating accidents, swimming activities, and accidental falls into water. In wilderness settings, 85 percent of fatal accidents involve water.

Some of us relax around water and feel comfortable using various types of water recreation activities in our youth ministries. Others see water as a dangerous element of God's creation and give it the utmost respect. This chapter will offer a balanced perspective by surveying several popular water recreation activities and raising safety concerns related to water recreation and youth ministry.

Water Safety Standards

The American Camping Association requires accredited camps offering aquatic programs to meet strict standards of certification for their water safety staff. How does your youth ministry measure up to these standards when you offer a water-related event?

Who is the lifeguard? Are you protected by a lifeguard who is certified by a respected training agency, such as the American Red Cross, the YMCA, Lifeguard BSA, or the Royal Lifesaving Bronze Medallion? Have the lifeguards demonstrated skill in rescue and emergency procedures specific to their situations? Are they trained and supervised to enforce established safety regulations, to provide necessary instruction, to identify and to manage environmental and other hazards related to the activity?

Who has emergency response skills? Is there at least one staff member present and accessible with these certifications: American Red Cross Standard First Aid (or its equivalent) and CPR for the age level, certified by the American Red Cross, the American Heart Association, or an equivalent?

What preparations have you made?

■ Have you listed specific safety rules for your water-related activity? Do you orient students to the safety rules and procedures prior to the activity?

■ Do you have written procedures for emergency and accident responses? Are these procedures rehearsed periodically?

■ Are kids tested for swimming ability before they are allowed to participate in aquatic activities?

■ Do the lifeguards and lookouts have a system that enables them to quickly account for all participants?

■ Is rescue equipment readily available and in good condition?

The best water safety preparation we youth leaders can make is to have our youth swim under the supervision of a certified lifeguard. As adult leaders, we must defer to the judgment and leadership of the lifeguard in matters of water safety and support the lifeguard before our students. When we operate without a certified lifeguard, we take the heavy responsibility of safety upon ourselves. In either situation, however, the general rules of swimming safety apply.

Safety Tips for Swimming

■ Know your swimming abilities. Don't test yourself or others in situations beyond your skills.

■ Never swim alone. Use a buddy system.

■ Never swim close to any areas designated for sailboats or motor boats.

■ Never dive until you are sure the water is sufficiently deep and the bottom is free of hazardous objects.

■ Don't use flotation devices or water toys that might allow you to be carried far out into deep water.

■ Never try to swim against a strong current. Drift with it

and swim diagonally across it.

■ When caught in an undertow (shorter and deeper than a current), turn and go with it, swimming a diagonal course to the surface.

■ After sunset, swim only in well-lighted areas.

■ At the first flash of lightning, exit the water immediately.

■ Follow instructions from lifeguards. Respect their decisions. Never fake an emergency.

If there are students in your youth ministry who cannot swim, a lasting gift to them for life would be to teach them. Make it a goal to have every student in your group become a competent swimmer. In addition, encourage some of your student leaders to take lifeguard training offered by the Red Cross or YMCA. These organizations could provide your group with top quality safety coverage while developing kids' life skills.

Public and Private Pools

Public pools with certified lifeguards on duty make your safety job easy. Private pools in the homes of your friends or youth group members put the safety responsibility back into your hands. You can minimize your risks by following these guidelines:

■ Never allow swimming unattended by a trained adult.

■ Forbid running, pushing, and fighting around the pool.

■ Beware of the diving board. Use it with caution.

■ Don't overload the pool.

■ Don't allow students to jump on top of others.

■ Forbid "chicken fighting" (riding on a person's shoulders).

■ Don't allow anyone to be held under water.

■ Keep electrical devices away from the pool. Make sure that electrical outlets are equipped with ground-fault switches.

■ Keep emergency response equipment and phone numbers handy.

Lakes and Ponds

■ Never allow swimming unattended by a trained adult.

■ Check the bottom of the lake or pond for hazardous debris.

■ Establish and enforce a designated swimming area.

■ Allow no diving without first checking the depth of the water.

■ Warn kids of the dangers of pushing or fighting on the rafts.

■ Know where you can get emergency assistance quickly.

The Ocean

■ Swim only under the supervision of a lifeguard. Swim near the lifeguard stand.

■ Stay away from piers and pilings.

■ Look out for dangerous aquatic life such as stinging coral and jellyfish.

■ Don't try to swim against strong currents. To make it back to shore, swim gradually away from the current.

■ Follow the lifeguards' instructions regarding surf conditions.

Canoeing, Rafting, and Tubing

For the best results and the safest conditions in these activities, find a reputable outfitter and arrange for the equipment, training, and supervision you need. Conditions can vary widely from flat, slow moving water to a fast, rapid-filled river. Obviously, the deeper and faster the water, the greater the risk.

Canoeing safety checklist. To make sure that your canoe trip is as safe as possible, adhere to the following guidelines:

■ Wear personal flotation devices (life jackets) at all times. Cushions are not reliable. Personal flotation devices safe for use must be U.S. Coast Guard-approved and of the proper type, size, and fit for each user.

■ Flotation devices must be worn snug and tight. Loose flotation devices are dangerous because they can hold a person underwater.

■ Be sure that everyone in the canoes can swim.

■ Notify several people or officials of your trip route and of your estimated time of return.

■ Stick to your planned route. If you change your plans, rescuers and other concerned parties will have difficulty finding you if you have an accident or other trouble.

■ Don't go into wilderness country without a map or magnetic compass. Islands and lakes all look alike. Portage trails seem to disappear if you don't watch the signs carefully.

■ Never run a stretch of rapids or white water without knowing exactly what lies ahead. Walk along the fast stretch to check the conditions before you attempt to run the river. If you have the least doubt you can make it safely, portage the canoes.

■ Never stand up in a canoe. It is safer to change places by going ashore to do so.

■ Carry a properly stocked first aid kit and know how to use it.

■ Be sure each canoe is in proper balance. Don't overload it. The middle section of the canoe should be at least six inches above the waterline.

■ Always keep a bailing can and a large sponge aboard to remove excess water from the bottom of the canoe.

■ If you are caught in a squall, sit in the bottom of the canoe; if conditions warrant it, lie flat on the bottom in such a position that you can bail.

■ If the canoe capsizes, hold on to the canoe and kick-swim it to shore. Canoes are buoyant and will float. It is safer to stay with the canoe than to attempt to swim ashore.

■ Learn how to right an upset canoe in the water. Learn how to re-enter a swamped canoe.

■ At the first sign of lightning, get out of the water and away from a metal canoe. Wait out the storm in a nearby shelter or under small trees.

■ Avoid swinging the canoe paddles to splash another canoe.

■ Avoid taking a long straight course across a lake. Storms can come up quickly, so stay close to shore.

■ Always take along a staff member with the American Red Cross Standard First Aid certification (or equivalent) and CPR certification (the American Red Cross, the American Heart Association, or an equivalent) for the appropriate age level.

In a deep, fast river. In white water, all canoeists should wear helmets to protect their heads from rocks and debris, if their craft should capsize. They should avoid being in the water downstream from their canoes. The water will push the canoe toward them with tremendous force. If they become pinned against something in the river, a canoe could do them great injury. Take great caution when trees and branches are down in the river. The force of the river can push canoeists who are in the water up against these obstructions, causing hypothermia or drowning.

Staff supervision of a canoe trip. The maximum size for a safe canoe trip is eight to twelve canoes (with two people in each canoe). Assign three or four leaders or guides to specific positions among the canoes. One leader should be at the front, and no canoe should be allowed to pass the leader's canoe. Place two experienced leaders in the middle of the group to supervise and monitor the students in the canoes. A fourth leader should stay in the rear of the group to act as a sweeper and to ensure everyone's safe passage.

These leaders should be selected on the basis of their canoeing experience, their knowledge of the river, and their demonstrated abilities to control a group of four canoes (eight young people). Each leader's canoe should carry a first aid kit and a set of ropes with ring buoys to throw to people as lifelines. If at all possible, take the leaders on a pretrip run to build their knowledge of the river and to give them experience communicating with each other while they are actually canoeing.

Before you leave. Pretrip training in an indoor facility is highly recommended for students as well as staff. Make the pool training part of the entire trip package. Lay out the rules of the trip. Use the life jackets and the paddles. Give basic instruction in all aspects of canoeing, including stroking and righting a capsized canoe. The pool setting also provides opportunity to test swimming skills and teach safety techniques in a controlled setting. The training process gives insight into the teachable attitude of each student. The pool training may eliminate some kids from the trip. If they can't take instruction in the pool, don't expect them to cooperate when everyone is moving down a river.

Rafting and tubing. Because of several fatal tragedies, white-water rafting has recently been under a great deal of scrutiny from the insurance industry. Although these accidents were on dangerous Class V rivers, every rafting outfitter has been placed under similar scrutiny. The job of the youth leader is to find a top-notch outfitter with good equipment to guide the youth group.

Many of the safety guidelines listed for canoeing apply to rafting. Listen to the instructions of your outfitter. Let the company do the work and provide the safety precautions for which you are paying.

Be sure to check the liability insurance policy of your church or youth ministry to see if it excludes white-water rafting. Work with the outfitter to make sure each participant is adequately covered by insurance.

Tubing should be limited to slow, lazy rivers on hot summer days. It is impossible to control a tube and thus to protect arms and legs (and other vulnerable areas of the body) in a fast river with rocks. Even if participants wear helmets, the injury risk is beyond what is acceptable for a youth ministry. In addition, although you are on a slow river, everyone must be a strong swimmer. The leaders must know the river (Is there a waterfall ahead?) and be strategically placed throughout the group as specified earlier.

A final warning. Youth leaders should not sign a group waiver form and take responsibility for all the students. When the river outfitter requires waivers releasing them from any responsibility, get the forms prior to the trip. Give these forms to the students to be signed by their parents and notarized.

In a lawsuit that is still pending, a youth leader and the ministry who employs him is being sued by the family of a young person who was killed during a rafting trip. The leader signed the waiver form for the river company at the site just before they left on the trip. His signature said that he and his ministry organization would take responsibility for the students. Lack of planning and a spur-of-the-moment decision caused the youth leader to take the responsibility that belonged only to the parents. He and his ministry are awaiting the judgment of the courts.

Water-Skiing and Boating

Late one afternoon at a Christian camp, a full-time, experienced water safety staff member broke his own rules of safety. He had been driving the water-ski boat for over four hours (rule number one) and was feeling the fatigue. This last ride was with a good friend who was asking for more and more challenges. He accommodated his friend's requests and took him off the normal ski course (rule number two). Driving into an area of the lake restricted to sailboats (rule number three), he crashed his boat directly into a sailboat.

The occupants of the sailboat had seen him coming and

had dived off the boat into the water. A young woman from the sailboat was just ascending to the surface when the propeller of the motorboat passed her. The young woman sustained deep lacerations to her back. The water safety staff member immediately stopped the boat and switched into the emergency response mode in which he had been trained. Miraculously, the young woman lived and recovered.

What Causes Water Accidents?

■ ■ ■ ■ ■ ■ ■

■ Alcohol and drug use while participating in water recreation

■ Diving into unknown waters or water that is too shallow

■ Overestimating one's ability and stamina

■ Sudden immersion (falls into water)

■ Medical emergencies such as heart attacks and seizures

(American Red Cross)

■ ■ ■ ■ ■ ■ ■

Following the accident, the camp staff review determined that this highly trained, mature leader had become the victim of fatigue. He was so familiar with the water that he overlooked the risks of skiing outside the designated areas. Familiarity had bred contempt for the risk. He got caught up in his relationship with a friend who wanted to push the limits of his skiing ability. It was a lapse of maturity on the leader's part to accommodate his friend.

This leader bears a resemblance to many youth ministry workers. He was diligent and hard-working. He had been in the driver's seat four hours without relief. He was like most youth ministers—highly motivated and unable to tell when it was time to quit. He was also highly relational, eager to meet any request of a friend. All together in this situation, his strengths became his weaknesses. Fortunately for him, the young woman's recovery freed him from having to carry an enormous weight of guilt the rest of his life.

Boating safety checklist. If a mature professional can experience a safety lapse such as this, it should serve as a warning to the rest of us who use boats only occasionally. If your youth ministry plans to use a boat for any activities, you are responsible to ensure that the boat meets basic safety requirements.

You may be looking at a boat owned by a camp you are using or a borrowed boat loaned to you for youth ministry use. Check the boat and the driver before you trust your young people to step on board. In particular, be sure to follow these guidelines:

■ Know the capabilities of your boat and motor.

■ Know your fuel tank capacity. Monitor fuel levels frequently so you don't become stranded.

■ Don't overload your boat. Balance your load.

■ Always have firefighting and lifesaving equipment ready to use.

■ Obey all boating laws and regulations.

■ Provide personal flotation devices for every person in the boat. (This is the law.)

■ Require all children to wear life preservers. Everyone else must wear them in rough weather.

■ Prepare for emergencies such as a fire, someone overboard, bad leaks, a motor breakdown, or a storm.

■ Learn distress and other marine signals.

■ Carry proper charts and a magnetic compass.

■ Have at least one person on board prepared to act as emergency co-pilot.

■ Follow manufacturer's specifications regarding the number of passengers you can safely carry.

■ Make sure that everyone in the boat is seated before the motor is started.

■ Drive at below-average speeds in unfamiliar waters to reduce the possibility of striking an unexpected obstacle.

■ Watch for swimmers at all times.

■ Know the official storm signals. Boat accordingly.

■ When it appears that a storm is possible, head for home without delay.

■ Angle your boat toward high waves and reduce your speed.

- Avoid unnecessarily fast, sharp turns. Don't risk being swamped or capsized by high waves.

- If the boat capsizes, passengers should try to stay with it. The overturned boat can support quite a few people even if it is nearly underwater.

- Guard against panic in an emergency. Calmness, co-operation, and resourcefulness are required for survival.

Water-skiing safety considerations. Water-skiing is popular with many youth ministries. It provides opportunity to build relationships and to share an exhilarating experience. It is most safely operated in the context of an accredited camp. Other youth ministries use boats periodically in local settings. To involve more kids, boats also pull young people on knee boards and inflated inner tubes. The following safety considerations apply to all these variations.

- Know and follow the state laws governing boating and skiing.

- Ski in safe areas that are free from shallow rocks and other obstructions.

- Load the ski boat with enough forward ballast to hold down the bow and to guarantee forward vision. The safety of the skier depends upon where the boat takes him or her.

- Always place a trained adult spotter in the boat to watch the skier and communicate with the driver. Many states also require the boat to have a rearview mirror in addition to a spotter. Check your state's requirements.

- Insist that all skiers wear legal life jackets. Know what type of life jacket the law requires.

- Use a standard set of signals for communications between boat and skier.

- Remember that the boat can slow down faster than a skier can.

- When ending a run, slow down gradually before shutting off the engine. This will protect the skier from being driven into the boat by his or her momentum.

- Watch for swimmers and hazards when skiing near a beach. Stay away from congested shore areas.
- Avoid towing skiers through heavily traveled or congested areas.
- Teach skiers to grab one ski and hold it vertically out of the water when they fall so that other boats can see them in the water. Do the same with a knee board.
- Stop the boat motor (don't just switch to neutral) when taking a skier on board.
- Never tow your skier through shallow waters at high speeds. A tumble could be hazardous.
- Never tow two or more tubes or knee boards with students of significantly different weights or with different lengths of rope. The longer rope can decapitate the person holding on to the shorter rope.
- Terminate water-skiing well before twilight, when visibility decreases.
- Inspect towlines and fastenings regularly for worn or damaged equipment.

Water Safety Training

The American Red Cross, YMCA, YWCA, and other organizations offer water safety courses and comprehensive training for leaders. Textbooks and practical instruction will give leaders confidence in handling safety procedures and emergency responses around water activities. Contact the local office of these organizations in your community or the national headquarters listed in the appendix (p. 234).

Winter Water Sports

"Wake up, Jack! Steven is hurt. He ran into the tree, and he can't move." I couldn't decide if the voice was coming from my dreams or from reality. I opened my eyes to see

It Was Just a Short Trip to the Dock

■ ■

It was late in the afternoon. Four hours of water-skiing and tubing were coming to an end. The staff leader had given every student the opportunity for a great ride. As he prepared to move the motorboat to its overnight docking location, several young men begged for one more ride on the tubes (pulled water-ski style) over to the dock. The staff leader relented and gave them the go-ahead. They each grabbed a tube and a rope and hung on as the boat swung out into deep water and around to the dock.

During the short trip, one of the young men lost his grip on the rope and tube. Not wearing a life preserver, he slipped below the surface of the water. When the leader realized he was missing, he returned the boat to the spot where he disappeared into the water.

The staff leader faced a major dilemma. He wasn't alone in the boat. He had brought his three-year-old son with him for this short trip to tie up the boat. Should he dive into the water for the drowning young man and leave his young son unsupervised in a boat in deep water? He chose to stay in the boat with his son. Tragically, the young man drowned. He was a nonswimmer riding a tube in deep water without a life jacket.

The leader made several poor decisions that set the stage for this tragedy. First, he decided to take his infant son in the boat without any other supervision. Second, he consented to the request for one last tube ride to students who weren't prepared (no life jackets). Third, he assumed that everyone hanging on to the ropes of the boat could swim.

All these decisions were made quickly and casually. Understandably, the leader wanted to please everyone (his son and the young men). But what should have been the most routine movement of the boat turned into a tragedy he will never forget.

■ ■ ■ ■ ■ ■ ■ ■ ■ ■ ■ ■ ■ ■ ■ ■ ■ ■ ■ ■

kids dressed in ski jackets and mittens hovering over me, begging me to get up and come with them. I asked where Steven was. I sent one young man to wake another counselor from the group (I was just a weekend visitor) and gave the students a blanket to wrap around Steven. I cautioned them not to move him but to tell him I would be there as soon as I got dressed.

What time was it? I squinted through my sleepy eyes to see 3 a.m. glaring back at me. I knew I had to dress for cold weather. The temperature had been barely above zero all weekend. It had to be at least fifteen degrees below zero now. I prayed for Steven as I dressed and asked God to show me what I needed to do when I arrived at the scene of the accident.

When I walked out of the camp dormitory to the sledding hill, I was surprised to find no one at the hill or near the tree where they told me Steven was lying. After searching the area, I returned to the building to find Steven in his bed, surrounded by a roomful of kids. He had been sledding with all of them at 3 a.m. while the counselors were sound asleep. He had hit the tree headfirst. The impact caused temporary paralysis, which made it impossible for him to move for a few minutes. When the feeling had returned, he had gotten up off the ground and walked to his room.

As Steven lay in his bunk, he was sore, scared, and thankful the paralysis wasn't permanent. I was quite aggravated about the 3 a.m. sledding, but I was glad he wasn't still lying on the ground next to that tree. Soon the discussion turned to Steven's need to visit the hospital emergency room for a checkup. He said he was fine. That was "teen-speak" for "I don't want to explain to my parents why I was sledding at 3 a.m." He almost had several counselors convinced until I stepped in and demanded he be taken to the hospital. To my amazement, Steven suffered no serious damage or any side effects.

When the temperature drops and the water turns to snow and ice, youth ministry activities become even more exciting. Snow camps, winter retreats, ski trips, and ice skating parties help youth groups enjoy the cold weather. The safety demands for winter activities become intense, however, because the winter weather creates an environment filled with fast and slippery hard surfaces surrounded by cold temperatures.

Ice Sports

Ice skating is popular with youth groups throughout the year, for many go to indoor arenas. In most situations, the level of safety is acceptable because of the regulations and supervision provided by the operators of the rink. When the youth ministry moves away from the rink and onto a pond or lake, keeping young people safe becomes more challenging.

■ Check the thickness of the ice. The Red Cross suggests that, for maximum safety, the ice should be at least four inches thick. Check the entire area you intend to use for sufficient thickness. The more people you put on the ice, the thicker it needs to be. Mark off areas where the ice is not sufficiently thick as "restricted" areas.

■ Look for objects or other hazards that stick out above the ice. Mark them so they can be avoided.

■ Always have something you can throw or extend to a person who has fallen though the ice. It could be a long pole or a lifeline with a buoy. Prepare for the worst and hope you never have to use such devices.

■ If the ice starts to crack, lie down flat on the ice, spreading your hands and legs far apart to distribute your weight across a wide area. Crawl toward the safer, thicker ice while maintaining your prone, spread position. Do not stand up until you are safely on solid ground.

How to help someone who has fallen through the ice. Don't go out onto the ice to help. You may join the person in the cold water if you do. Extend an emergency device, such as a long pole, a tree branch, a buoy on a lifeline, or an inner tube tied to a rope, that the victim can grasp and hold on to.

Get something to the person quickly. The longer the victim is in the cold water, the less he or she will be able to function. Pull the victim to shore or get the victim attached to the rescue device and go for help.

Coach the victim to remain calm and to reach forward onto the ice, using a swimming-type kick to push up onto the ice. The victim should stay prone on the ice, distributing his or her weight, then crawl or roll away from the hole in the ice.

Get the victim into dry clothes and a warm shelter as quickly as possible. Warm the person with a warm (not hot) shower or bath or by placing him or her near a fire. Give the person warm liquids, but avoid alcohol or caffeine. Wrap the person in dry clothes, a blanket, or a sleeping bag. Get medical assistance, if possible.

More ice problems. Many youth ministers believe that games on ice are even more fun than on solid ground. It is not unusual to see broom hockey, ice hockey, football, soccer, and all types of relay races on ice. The problem is that ice is as hard as concrete. Young people who fall are often injured. If the professional hockey leagues require helmets for safety of the players, should less-coordinated kids participate in contact sports on ice without head protection? Even with helmets, the students face a greater risk of broken bones playing on ice.

Fun in the Snow

We were promoting our winter snow camp with a film piece that showed more than twenty people sliding down a snow covered trail in the woods on ten inner tubes that had been lashed together. It was like a raft trip, only through the woods and over the snow. It looked like so much fun.

When we arrived at camp, we were anxious to duplicate what we had seen on the film. The camp had the snow, the inner tubes, and the long, downhill runs. The camp director assigned one of his trained staff to supervise our tube run. His rules were much different from what we expected or wanted. He allowed only one person on the tube at a time and only one tube on the course at a time. He placed some spotters along the course and at the bottom to help the rider exit the course and return up the hill. It seemed as though he was spoiling all the fun. In fact, when he would be called away for some task around the camp, we would defy the younger camp counselors and hook three or four tubes together, pile as many people on them as possible, and take a merry ride down the hill. It seemed like a lot more fun.

Since that weekend, we have used camps that have not provided professional supervision. We have had total freedom to do whatever we wanted with tubes, sled, and toboggans. Left to our own rules, we have discovered our camp director friend was pretty smart.

Most accidents on tubes, sleds, and toboggans happen when people hit other people—one body crashing into other bodies. You pile two people on top of a tube for a run down the hill. It is great fun until a bump sends one person's head into the teeth of a fellow passenger, or the bulk of one rider lands full force on an arm or a skinny leg of the other rider.

We loved to play Chicken with the people standing in the runway of the track. We hated to wait for people to clear the track. Most of our accidents and consequent hospital runs, however, were caused by people hitting others either deliberately or because they were out of control. We used to send riders down backward, but too many riders hit trees or other people because they had no idea where they were headed and had no ability to change direction.

You must ask yourself, as I did, if it is worth the risk of

Snowballs

■ ■

No youth leader wants to outlaw snowballs on a winter retreat. But why is it that a combination snowball and iceball always finds the face of someone who is not involved as a
thrower and is the least prepared to receive it? That's when
the leader blows his or her top and bans snowballs for the
rest of the weekend.

Be creative. Make special rules for snowballs and all those who
want to be throwers. Make it similar to registering a gun. Have
kids sign up as snowball throwers and accept the restriction to
throw only at other snowball throwers. Give throwers special,
brightly colored armbands to attach to their coats. Without the
armbands, they will not be allowed to throw any snowballs
without being disciplined. If they throw at or hit anyone without armbands, they can expect to lose their privileges.

Always try to find a way for kids to have fun without jeopardiz-
ing the safety of others.

■ ■

injury to continue a no-restraints approach to tubes, toboggans, and sleds. It is impossible to safety-proof these activities. Although most of us have done these activities since we
were kids, a safety check points out that accidents happen
because of the speed, the lack of control, and the exposure
of arms, legs, and heads to collisions. However, you can
minimize your risks by following a few safety guidelines:

■ Have a straight, wide course free of hazards and obstructions (including people).

■ Avoid using sleds and toboggans with metal runners
or metal facing that could cut someone's skin.

■ Allow just one rider on each tube and sled. Don't
overload large toboggans. Have all riders head down the hill
feet first.

■ Place staff leaders at the top and bottom of the hill to
spot for the students and to enforce the rules.

■ Discourage the building of jumps on the run. Being lifted in the air is fun, but landing on the ground is dangerous.

Snowmobile fun. Snowmobiles are excluded from many insurance policies because of the loose restrictions concerning their operation and the numerous accidents that involve them. Many camps still run snowmobiles under their own insurance policies, but they allow only qualified camp staff to operate the powerful vehicles. Both drivers and riders should always wear helmets.

In an attempt to be creative, some camps have snowmobiles pull campers on inner tubes, water-ski style. The terrain, though, is less predictable than a water surface. During the research for this book, several youth leaders reported that young people from their groups had hit trees when they were on tubes pulled by snowmobiles. One student suffered brain damage. Check your insurance policy before using snowmobiles. If you have coverage, use only qualified drivers, wear helmets, and obey all safety regulations.

Downhill skiing. One youth organization recently experienced an embarrassing day in the legal system. It was being sued by the family of a young man who had sustained a serious back injury while downhill skiing with the group. What was unique about this legal proceeding was that the episode in question had been recorded on a videotape shot by one of the youth group leaders.

The video clearly showed the young man was a novice skier trying to ski down a slope that was beyond his capabilities. He was skiing out of control and fell, injuring his back. Students and staff skiing with him could be heard encouraging him to ski down this slope and laughing when he fell. As he lay on the snow, they quipped and joked with him about getting up to continue skiing. In the context of the accident, the comments took on a different tone than was intended. The leaders sounded insensitive and unconcerned for his safety.

The judgment of the suit went against the youth organization.

A responsible skiing trip starts with staff preparations. You will need to get signed release forms and medical information for all the participants. In addition, it is smart to have at least one alternate driver riding with you in case one of the drivers suffers an injury during the day.

Ski trips often attract kids who don't know the group or leaders very well. They might not be able to identify who is responsible for them when they are asked by medical personnel. So give each person in your group a slip of paper with your name and the name of your group written on it. Emergency personnel can use this information to call for leaders over a public address system.

Set a meeting time during the day (a one-hour period) when each person should report to a staff person at a designated location. Set a quitting time and a meeting spot for departure. If possible, have an adult at a designated location throughout the day. Show students the location and instruct them to come to this person if they need any help during the day. That adult should also know how to contact the leader during the day if necessary.

If you travel by bus, have alternate transportation available if it is necessary to take a student to an emergency room.

Instruct students not to ski alone. Try to establish small groups of skiers to stay with each other and look out for each other. Try to get adult leaders spread out into all the various groups of skiers. Be sure that capable adult leaders are supervising the beginning skiers.

In extremely cold weather, instruct your students to return to the lodge to warm up after a certain period of time or number of runs. Alert students to the signs of frostbite, and warn them to get help from you or the infirmary before they develop a severe condition.

Make sure that all skiers wear goggles to protect their eyes from snow, ice, and damage caused by the sun.

Don't allow experienced skiers to take others onto ski trails that are beyond their skiing skills. Review the skiing safety code below.

- Ski under control and in such a way that you can stop or avoid other skiers or objects.

- When skiing downhill or overtaking another skier, you have the responsibility to avoid the skier below you.

- Do not stop where you obstruct a trail or are not visible from above.

- When you enter a trail or start downhill, yield to other skiers.

- Wear retention straps or other devices to help prevent runaway skis.

- Keep off closed trails and posted areas and observe all posted signs.

Four major causes of skiing injuries.

1. Lack of instruction. The goal of skiing instruction is to teach skiers how to control where they are going, how fast they are going, and how to stop safely. Every beginning skier needs instruction. The responsible leader will offer instruction either through professional lessons at the lodge's ski school or from capable volunteers in the youth group. Most ski-related injuries happen to beginning skiers. Many of those injuries take place on ski slopes that are much more challenging than the skiers are able to handle. It is important to take the time to teach beginners to ski under control. The throw-'em-in-the-deep-end method of teaching people to swim or ski is much too risky for a youth ministry leader.

Once I took a young man skiing who had never skied before. I was impatient and didn't want to spend all morning on the bunny slope. He was young and athletic. I was confident I could teach him on the way down the hill. Looking at the trail map, I found several green trails (the easiest) on the side of the mountain. When we left the chairlift at the top of the mountain, I discovered the green trails were closed. I was angry, but I had not taken time to check trail conditions before I took this novice skier up on the chairlift.

Now I was at the top of the lift with a young man who never skied before. Only blue (difficult) and black (expert) trails were open. The trip down was a real disaster for him. Falling constantly took away his energy and confidence. After fifteen minutes, he hated skiing. After he took a particularly nasty fall, I realized the danger I had put him in and flagged down a ski patrol. They called a sled to take him down to the base of the mountain and gave me a well-deserved reprimand. Then the young man and I spent the rest of the day on the bunny slope rebuilding his confidence and teaching him the basics.

The same pressure is applied to many young people by friends who have more skiing experience. They don't want to spend the day on the bunny slope. Forgetting what it takes to learn to ski, they take their friends onto difficult runs, where an accident happens and someone gets hurt. The leader then gets to spend the rest of the day in a first aid station or hospital emergency room. Prevent these accidents by demanding that beginning skiers stay on the bunny slope until they demonstrate an ability to ski under control.

2. Inadequate physical conditioning. Learning to ski can be very hard on young people who are not physically fit. Not everyone is ready for the rigors of skiing. Weaker people sustain more injuries. You need strong leg muscles and ligaments to withstand the forces of a fall. Stamina is needed to keep you from tiring quickly. Either prepare nonathletes before the trip or keep a staff leader nearby to monitor them while they ski.

3. Inadequate equipment. Good equipment that is properly fitted and adjusted reduces the possibility of injury. Resist the temptation to save equipment rental money by borrowing equipment for new skiers. The fit of the boots, the length of the skis and poles, and the release setting on the bindings are crucial to a skier's safety and comfort. When young people rent equipment, remind them to answer questions about their weight and their skiing abilities honestly. Their answers will determine how tightly the bindings that hold the boots to the skis will be tightened. They should not feel embarrassed or pressured into giving information that isn't true. A dishonest answer can result in a broken leg, if a ski doesn't release properly from the boot when the skier falls.

4. Lack of sound judgment. Beginning skiers have little conception of how great a hazard speed can be. They often overestimate their abilities and are deaf to instructions. The key to safety is skiing under control. Most accident victims tell the same basic story. "I just started going faster and faster. I didn't know how to stop." Or "My skis got crossed and I couldn't control where they were going."

Lack of sound judgment also causes people to ski past the point of exhaustion. The last run of the day is notorious for accidents. Skiers become fatigued and grow careless or unable to control their speed. Be careful not to verbally abuse the youth in your group when they say they are tired or want to quit for the day. Your comments may push them to ski beyond their physical limits. The leader bears some responsibility for any accidents to students not given an opportunity to rest or call it quits.

After a full day of skiing with a group of young people, the trip home offers additional safety challenges. The parking lot of the ski area can be hazardous. Tired students with aching feet don't always pay close attention to the traffic. Vehicles with snow or winter dirt on the windshield don't always have clear visibility. The light of the late afternoon is fading. Pay special attention to your group and to others around you to avoid any parking lot mishaps.

EIGHT

High Adventure

■ ■

Lenny slammed his bicycle down on the pavement of the parking lot. Walking quickly past the picnic table covered with sandwiches and drinks, he cursed everyone and everything in his path. Just two-and-a-half days into an eight-day, four hundred-mile bicycle trip, Lenny was coming apart. Upon reaching the side entrance of the park, he announced he was going home...and he started walking.

I calmly ate my lunch waiting for Lenny to return. When he was almost out of sight, I realized he was serious. My legs felt rubbery, but I ran down the road in pursuit. Lenny had no idea where he was or where he was going (a perfect illustration of his life). He was like a ticking time bomb rolling down the road. Nearly a mile later, I finally cornered him against a fence and attempted to calm and defuse him.

The peace treaty we negotiated was only temporary. Every day something else related to Lenny exploded. He collapsed from heat exhaustion because he insisted on riding with his jeans and jacket on. He sabotaged his own bike. He was in a fight almost every day. One incident came immediately after another student pulled Lenny out of a river when he appeared to be drowning. During a rainstorm, Lenny was riding so erratically that a leader separated him from the rest of the group. In anger, Lenny pulled a knife and threatened him.

Before the trip, I had thought that a high-adventure trip would help Lenny turn his life around. Now I wonder how

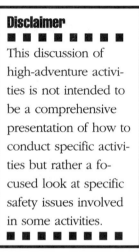

Disclaimer

■ ■ ■ ■ ■ ■ ■ ■

This discussion of high-adventure activities is not intended to be a comprehensive presentation of how to conduct specific activities but rather a focused look at specific safety issues involved in some activities.

■ ■ ■ ■ ■ ■ ■ ■

we ever survived that week. Today I realize that putting Lenny into a high-adventure situation threatened not only his safety but also the well-being of all the other students and staff.

What Is High Adventure?

High adventure is voluntarily putting ourselves into situations in the physical environment that challenge our physical and emotional toughness. High adventure is doing what is outside the boundaries of what most people would consider normal, safe activities.

High adventure includes mountaineering, ballooning, scuba diving, bicycling, motorcycling, canoeing, kayaking, rafting, sailing, skiing, hang gliding, sky diving, rock climbing, trekking, survival camping, and similar activities. This chapter offers general safety principles for use in these activities by a youth ministry. Special attention is given to bicycle touring and hiking or backpacking, with a short note about rock climbing and rappelling because they are often utilized in youth ministry. Check the chapter on water activities for additional comments.

Before Considering High Adventure

One word of advice fits all: High-adventure activities should never be attempted by someone lacking adequate training and experience. The smartest move any youth leader can make is to hire a certified trainer or guide to lead a youth group through one of these activities. If you are unwilling to spend the money to hire qualified guides, stay away from high adventure. Don't rush ignorantly into any high-adventure trips with a local amateur staff. It takes time to recognize the risks and to develop competence and experience in your leaders.

By definition, high-adventure trips are risky and dangerous. That's part of the appeal that leads many youth leaders to use them. These trips are stressful on people physically, emotionally, socially, and in every other way. Even if you follow the strictest safety standards, accidents will happen because these activities are conducted in a dangerous environment.

Questions Worth Asking

Why do I want to involve young people in high adventure? Is high adventure really necessary to accomplish your goals? The first step in planning any activity is writing a clear purpose statement for the activity. Perhaps there is a better and safer way to accomplish your goal. Exposing your young people to the risks of high adventure may be unnecessary.

Who is going to lead this high-adventure experience? Do you have the experienced and qualified leaders to safely lead this adventure, or will you hire professional guides? Quality leadership is the most important ingredient for both safety and success in high adventure.

What type of young people should participate? Was it wise to bring Lenny on the bicycle trip? Definitely not! Lenny was not ready, either physically, emotionally, or socially, for the stresses imposed by a four hundred-mile bicycle trip with thirty of his peers. You need to consider vital information about the young people you plan to take on high adventure.

■ What is their overall physical health?

■ What are their physical abilities and capabilities?

■ Do they have any drug or alcohol problems? High adventure is no place to go cold turkey.

■ Are they at all irrational or unpredictable? High adventure will only magnify it.

■ Are they cocky, ego-driven, reckless, or afraid to fail? If so, expect severe overreactions and poor response to leadership.

■ How do they act when under stress in their normal environments and routines? The answer is a reliable guide to how they will behave in high-adventure situations.

■ How well do they accept and follow instructions?

■ Are there scapegoat kids in your group, targets of peer abuse?

■ Is there time to screen students individually to determine how this trip might affect each person?

■ What training and conditioning will you provide prior to the trip to prepare the students?

Lenny came on the trip at the last minute because I insisted on taking him. He wasn't screened with these type of questions. We didn't know until after the trip that he had been kicked out of three schools for fighting. As much as we cared, we were not prepared to deal with him. The situation we thrust him into only aggravated his problems. Lenny became a major safety risk to himself and to others around him.

What is our true exposure to danger in this event? Experience is vital for risk to be fairly and accurately assessed. Most dangerous situations are repetitive and can be predicted by an experienced leader. As a youth leader, you must know what risks your students will face and decide if it is worth it. Those decisions are best made prior to departing, not in the heat of the moment.

What is the quality of the equipment we will use? It pays to go with a trained, certified outfitter who has quality equipment. It is seldom worth the investment for your group to buy specialty items for occasional use. High adventure requires top quality equipment. This is not the place for shortcuts or budget constraints.

How did my staff and I react when we went on a

AWOL
■ ■

He was gone! Jeff's heart raced as he circled the edge of the camp looking for any sign of Richie. Jeff had found Richie's sleeping bag empty and cold when he went to wake him. Jeff had spent two stormy days with Richie and his streetwise buddies, but he never dreamed that Richie would bolt from the group.

Jeff left the group in the hands of his well-trained assistant leader and set off double-pace, retracing the trail of the previous two days. Still no Richie. He hiked to the ranger station and reported his missing young man.

The next forty-eight hours were the longest of Jeff's life. Finally word came to Jeff and the remaining hikers. The ranger had word Richie was safe. He had caught on with another group of hikers and had walked off the mountain. When he hit the highway, he found a phone and called home for someone to pick him up.

Jeff now reflects that the wilderness was too intense for Richie. It was far beyond the comfort zone of his urban neighborhood. Introducing Richie to the wilderness should have been in shorter, less stressful doses. High adventure is not another trip to the mall or an amusement park. The natural environment poses numerous, serious threats to health and safety. It cannot be taken lightly.

■ ■

trial run? Before taking any students on a high adventure, have a qualified guide lead you and your adult leaders on a short sample of the high-adventure experience you are considering. Seeing, feeling, and touching it for yourself will help you decide if it is best for the students you serve. Use this time to teach your leaders needed skills in group process. Debriefing experiences are the primary teaching opportunities high-adventure trips offer. With the help of your staff, students can learn valuable lessons about themselves with regards to pressure, people, situations, fears, and faith.

What is our insurance coverage for this activity? Don't wait until you have an accident to ask this question. Your insurance agent does not want to be surprised with a claim for an event that your policy excludes. If you are working with a reputable outfitter, you should be able to arrange special coverage to protect everyone involved. Be sure that you have both medical and liability coverage for the trip. Seek the approval of your board or church leadership to confirm that you have sufficient insurance coverage.

Do parents know what kids will be doing? This is key. Parents need specifics (verbally and in writing) about what their young people will be experiencing on this trip. One of the major causes of lawsuits is surprise. Parents deserve prior knowledge. Put all the information on the permission form they will sign to give consent for the activity.

Training for Trips

Training for biking or hiking trips needs to start four to six weeks before the trip. A training schedule of dates and exercise activities should be published and sent to every registered participant.

Training dates should be held at least once a week and should increase in difficulty. Safety measures should be enforced as strictly as they would be on the actual trip. Real-trip conditions should be simulated (wearing hiking boots, carrying a loaded backpack, or shifting gears while riding up hills, for instance) to prepare a student's body for the new stresses of the trip.

Bicycle Trips

It was always a four-star, goose-flesh experience for

parents. The long double-line of bicycles, each marked with a fluorescent orange flag, coasted down the paved road into the picnic area of the state park, marking the end of a six hundred-mile trip. Parents and relatives would rush from the picnic tables to line the road and each look for that special face of their child.

The bikers would roll through a gauntlet of flashcubes, videotape cameras, and spirited applause before stopping to dismount and walk back into normal life. Mothers would breathe a big sigh of relief. We had arrived home safely. Fathers would beam with pride (especially for their daughters). It was a memorable moment of satisfaction and relief. For me, it was mostly relief.

Biking with young people has provided some of the great joys of my life and, sadly, the greatest sorrow I have ever known. (More about this later.) Genuine risk is always present. Despite the most thoughtful and strict safety standards, accidents will happen. Any leader considering biking with his or her youth group must count the potential cost.

I understand and respect parents who do not want their sons or daughters biking on a public roadway. The setting is filled with many uncontrollable elements. Our goal as youth leaders is to provide such an atmosphere of safety that parents can be confident each rider is safer with our group than if he or she were riding alone.

Bicycling Safety Essentials

The essentials of bicycle safety on public highways are the same no matter how long or short a trip you are on. There is no difference between a two-week tour or a one-day training ride near your home; the following requirements still apply:

Leadership. As always, good leaders are the key element of safe conduct. One riding leader for every three to five student riders is the best ratio. A group of six kids can be adequately supervised by one junior leader (an experienced college-age or less-experienced adult) *and* one senior leader (an experienced adult).

Good leaders possess riding experience, physical conditioning, basic leadership skills, and commitment to the standards of safety. The absence of any of these qualifications significantly raises the risk of accidents and injuries. Being responsible for the safety of biking students is not the place for on-the-job training.

Riding group size. The ideal size for biking is six to eight people, including leaders. Having more people in a group creates supervision difficulties, hinders communication, and becomes a hazard to other vehicles. Larger groups are socially more fun but significantly raise the probability of accidents. Stay small. It's safer. The size of the entire group will be determined by the number of qualified leaders you have and the capacity of your accommodations. Trips of thirty to forty people seem to work best.

Safety equipment and preparation. Before you and your students hit the road, make sure that you have the required equipment:

Helmets are an absolute must. Don't let anyone ride one hundred feet without wearing a quality biking helmet. The highest percentage of fatal accidents in biking are caused by severe head injuries. Stand firm and accept no excuses: No helmet, no riding. Check the helmet of each rider to make sure it rests squarely on the head, protecting the front and rear portions of the head. All chin straps must be fastened and drawn tight when riding. The helmet should be comfortable, but the rider should not be able to move it up and down or from side to side on the head. You can always expect resistance from some who don't want to wear helmets properly or at all. Remind them that they will probably only need that helmet once during their lifetimes, but that one moment could be the difference between a long life and a short one.

Cracked Heads

■ ■ ■ ■ ■ ■ ■ ■ ■ ■ ■ ■ ■ ■ ■ ■ ■ ■ ■ ■

Requiring bicycle helmets isn't much of a controversy today. I remember the day I changed my mind. Having ridden so many years and miles without a helmet, wearing one seemed unnecessary to me.

On this memorable day approximately one-third of our fifty riders were wearing helmets. We were cruising down a hill on a wide paved shoulder of the road into a small Connecticut town. Suddenly a car lurched out of the parking lot of a shopping center and stopped on the shoulder to check for oncoming traffic. The young driver didn't see us just thirty feet away and moving 22 to 24 miles per hour down the hill.

Brian, a 16-year-old on his first bike trip, was leading the group. He had no chance to stop his bike. When he hit the side of the car, the bike frame folded up like an accordion. Brian flipped over the front hood of the car and landed head first on the pavement. But the impact cracked open his helmet, not his head. Brian got up off the pavement scraped, bruised, scared...and alive.

That was the last year wearing helmets was voluntary. Some situations are absolutely unavoidable. If you are going to ride a bike on the road, you will encounter those unavoidable situations when a helmet could mean the difference between life and death.

■ ■ ■ ■ ■ ■ ■ ■ ■ ■ ■ ■ ■ ■ ■ ■ ■ ■ ■ ■

Fluorescent orange flags on six-foot-long fiberglass rods make bikes visible from all directions. They attach with brackets to the rear axles of bikes, or they can be taped to rear carrying racks. In general, flags, poles, and brackets can be obtained from bike dealers or major department stores for five to ten dollars each. Encourage each student to buy a flag for his or her bike, or provide the flags when kids show up for each ride. Quick-release axles make the flags easy to attach and detach.

Many young people initially resist riding with these flags because they associate them with children's bikes. Admittedly, most serious adult bikers don't use flags. Still, the flag requirement is valid. The flag gives drivers earlier visibility of the bikers. Drivers moving at the speed limit see bikers with flags three to five seconds earlier. That gives drivers additional time to adjust to the bikers' presence on the road by either slowing down or giving them more space.

You can't force students to ride with flags on their own personal time. You may not even want to use one during your personal riding. However, leading a group sponsored by a church or youth organization is a different matter. Provide the best possible safety. It may be the protection you need on the road and in a courtroom. When everyone in the group is required to use a flag and recognizes the leader is firm about it, the resistance usually disappears.

Bicycle inspection should be required before every trip. Ask an experienced bike mechanic to help check each bike. Not only will you be able to correct problems so that bikes run smoother and easier, you can also check essential safety items such as condition of tires and brakes. Participants can also be counseled about the quality and condition of their bikes in light of the trip they are planning to make with the group.

Safety standards for your biking group should be printed and made available for distribution to bikers and parents prior to the trip. Use the printed information as a basis for a verbal instruction about biking standards and practices for your group. Don't skip your safety standards orientation if a new student joins your group at the last minute. Don't assume that the student knows how to ride safely. Protect yourself and everyone in the group (including the new rider) with your safety orientation. Someday you may be asked by a lawyer to describe what safety instructions you gave to a student who was injured while biking under your supervision. Fight the temptation to take shortcuts in safety training.

It's Not Her Fault, Officer!

■ ■ ■ ■ ■ ■ ■ ■ ■ ■ ■ ■ ■ ■ ■ ■ ■ ■ ■ ■

Our biking group was pedaling up a long hill on a sweltering day. Lisa started to hyperventilate. The more she gasped for oxygen, the less she inhaled into her lungs. The feeling of suffocation caused her to panic and lose her balance; she fell off her bike into the grass on the side of the road. The leader took immediate control of the situation and quickly had Lisa breathing slowly and deeply into a "tent" made from a bandanna.

A well-meaning motorist passing by had seen Lisa fall and used his cellular phone to call an ambulance to the scene. When the ambulance arrived with an additional firetruck and two police cars, Lisa thought she was going to die from embarrassment. The medical team was very sharp and began to determine if she had suffered any head injuries when she fell. They asked Lisa some simple questions: Did she know where she was? What town she was in? What time was it? What day was it?

While the paramedics believed that the questions they were asking were simply routine, Lisa couldn't have answered any of those questions, even before she hyperventilated and fell. Like every other student in the group, she was just riding her bike with the group toward Boston. She had lost all track of time and dates.

No amount of explanation from the leader could change the mind of the medical team, who ordered her to be taken by ambulance to the hospital for observation. All the leader could do was keep his mouth shut and respect the decision of the medical team. She was released later that day.

■ ■ ■ ■ ■ ■ ■ ■ ■ ■ ■ ■ ■ ■ ■ ■ ■ ■ ■

Remember to supply this safety information to the parents prior to the trip.

Training rides are essential to prepare students for the trip. Review instructions on how to shift gears. If your planned trip will be through hilly or mountainous regions and the students live in a flat area, make your training strenuous and creative to prepare kids for what they will face. Set a minimum number of miles a student should ride prior to the trip. Be sure to strictly enforce the safety rules on training rides.

Selecting the route of the trip is best accomplished by sending out a scout team to drive several possible routes. The scouts should record in a notebook all the road conditions, directions, and places of interest bikers might stop during a riding day. Check state maps for recommendations about which roads are best for biking. Often, the state department of transportation can supply that information as well as warn you about narrow roads with high-speed and truck traffic. Once you have collected all this information, prepare printed directions outlining each day's route. Be sure to warn riders of any dangerous sections of highway. The sheet can also list information about emergency phone numbers, medical facilities, and each day's destination (with phone number).

Biking Safety Standards

■ Make safety your primary concern for you and for the members of your group. Obey all traffic rules just as you would driving a car. Ride single file just to the right of the solid line along the side of the road.

■ Communicate with the riders in your group. Riding in a group is different from riding alone. Riding behind another bike blocks your vision of approaching road conditions. Use a "call system" to inform each other of any obstacles, safety hazards, turns, needs to brake, or stops. The lead rider should call out the message. Each rider should re-peat the call until it is passed back to the last rider in the group. The last rider can call out any messages about ap-proaching traffic so riders can maintain their safe, single file formation as cars and trucks pass by. This call system will help you avoid accidents, flat tires, and bent rims.

■ Be ready for dangerous road conditions and try to avoid them at all times. Avoid riding across potholes, large cracks, and grooves in the road. Any of these can cause a biker to lose his or her balance. In wet weather, be aware of the additional braking time you will need. Rain and water off the tires also impairs vision. Slow down and put more space between the bikes. Constantly watch for changes in road conditions. Call out any broken glass, sand, gravel, dead animals, and other road debris.

■ When in heavy traffic, anticipate any hazard that could occur in a split second, such as a person in a parked car opening a door. Bikes don't handle well on steel-grated bridges (wet or dry), so slow down and ride cautiously. Watch your speed when going downhill. Spread out and put more space between the bikes. Allow more time to stop. Watch for traffic lights and stop signs at the bottoms of hills. Warn everyone riding behind you.

■ Never overlap wheels. Overlapping wheels is the greatest cause of serious accidents in group bike riding. Leaders must be relentless in enforcing this rule. Overlap-ping takes place when the front wheel of one bike is paral-lel or side by side with any portion of the rear wheel of the bike in front of it. In this situation, the wheels are so close together that any movement from side to side by either bike can cause the wheels to touch. Even the slightest brush of wheels can cause a rider (usually the rider following) to lose balance and become involved in an accident. Always keep a distance of at least two feet between the back tire of the lead bike and the front tire of the following bike. Increase this distance in hazardous conditions such as steep down-hills and wet roads. Riders should consistently and loudly call out braking and stopping situations to prevent bikers following from overlapping.

■ Ride as a group. Stay together as a group in all circumstances. Find a pace that everyone can keep. Don't let kids become separated by large gaps of space. Make every turn or lane change as a group, with the lead rider and rear rider checking the approaching traffic and calling out directions. Use hand signals to warn vehicles of your intentions. No one should turn or change lanes apart from the group. Move through traffic lights and intersections together as a group as well. The senior leader in a group is best positioned in the last spot of the line where he or she can see the entire biking group. Another leader can take one of the first three positions in the line.

■ Don't permit any foolish moves. What may seem safe when you bike individually is not safe for group riding. No riding without one's hands on the handlebars. No drafting of other vehicles. No weaving. No squirting water bottles at others, especially toward bikers who are passing. The natural response of the bike rider being squirted at is to swerve left, away from the water...and into traffic. Don't allow riders to wear headphones. Their hearing is key to their safety.

■ When you stop for repairs, directions, food, or even an accident, it is important to get off the road immediately. Every bike and rider should be as far onto the shoulder of the road as possible. If you stop where there is little or no shoulder, move to a different spot where riders can safely wait off the road while the problem is addressed.

Severe weather offers another reason to get the group entirely off the road. The presence of fog, heavy rain, and lightning require the group leader to make a decision. Consider the ability of drivers moving at highway speed to see the group and avoid striking any of the bikers. If there is any danger, be cautious and get off the road immediately until the weather conditions improve.

Get off the road when the traffic conditions, the condition of the road, or a combination of the two give you reason to believe that a biker might fall into traffic or be hit by a vehicle. No cyclist likes to walk his or her bike, but walking a bicycle on a bad road beats riding in an ambulance or a hearse. The leader cannot be afraid to make this decision (no matter how unpopular) and stick with it.

■ Never ride in darkness. No group should bike before sunrise or after sunset. Leaders should take note of sunset times and pull their groups off the road if they have not reached their destination. Take no chances in dusk light. Alternate transportation can be arranged. Be sure you have the phone number of where your group is staying so you can call for assistance.

Signs of Trouble

When is it unsafe for a student to ride? A well-trained leader can recognize trouble by carefully observing the bikers under his or her supervision. Here's a partial list of potentially dangerous situations.

Fatigue. Everyone gets tired on a bicycle trip; it's the leader's responsibility to monitor that fatigue and provide appropriate rest. When heads are consistently down and riders seem less alert, they are becoming tired. Fatigue makes bikers prime candidates for an accident. If students are not in good physical condition for the trip, arrange for them to ride only a portion of the day until they increase their strength and stamina. Fatigue is also the product of not enough sleep. Failure to enforce a curfew or allow enough sleep at night can lead to accidents on the road during the day. The longer the trip (in miles or in days), the greater the possibility of accumulated fatigue affecting the group.

Faintness, dizziness, or drowsiness. These threaten a rider's balance and ability to react. Leaders need to remind riders to speak up when they are experiencing these symptoms. Hot days, bright sun, dehydration, upset stomachs, and even medication can cause these symptoms. Encourage students to speak openly about how they feel. Ask them directly if they feel any symptoms. Respond immediately by getting afflicted riders off the road and into your support vehicle. Also, be aware of students using medications that cause drowsiness during the day.

Dehydration and heat problems. To replace body fluids, riders should drink regularly while they cycle. Every bike should carry one or two water bottles filled with water or with a sports exercise drink containing electrolyte supplements. Riders should take a drink every five or ten minutes, not waiting until they are thirsty to begin drinking. The leader should remind students to drink as they ride. A reliable guide for detecting dehydration is the inability to urinate at least every two hours while actively exercising. If someone cannot urinate every two hours, his or her body is holding on to fluids. This condition is easier to prevent than correct. Teach kids this warning sign of dehydration and encourage them to speak up about how they feel.

Heat exhaustion is caused by the body's loss of important fluids and salt. The signs and symptoms are dizziness, pale skin, nausea, and rapid heartbeat. Treat such victims by removing them from the heat source, sponging them down with water, and giving them sips of fluid fortified with an electrolyte supplement or salt. Be careful not to send sufferers into hypothermia during the cooling process.

Heat stroke is far more dangerous and arises much more quickly than heat exhaustion. Common symptoms are confusion, irrational behavior, rapid pulse and breathing, hot and dry skin, and loss of consciousness. To treat this condition, remove some of the person's clothing and moisten his or her body with cool water. Again, do not cool the body into a hypothermic state. Evacuation to a hospital is necessary.

Hyperventilation. When riders are climbing long hills, inhaling and exhaling heavily, they can develop shallow breathing patterns that don't provide enough oxygen to their systems. The faster they breathe, the less oxygen they actually get into their systems. They often panic, feeling a form of suffocation as they gasp for air. The leader must get such riders off the bike and seated in a safe spot, with their heads down between their knees. In ideal circumstances, the leader should put a paper bag over the victim's nose and mouth and instruct the victim to breath deeply and slowly. Lacking a paper bag, an inventive leader might use a bandanna, hold a shirt tent-style, or cup his or her hands over the student's nose and mouth. The victim needs more carbon dioxide in the lungs to restore normal breathing. The victim should rest until breathing returns to normal and he or she feels confident enough to get back on the bicycle.

Sunburn. Moving through the wind, riders may not realize the burn that the sun is putting on their skin. In addition to the normal spots that you expect to be sunburned, special care should be given to protect the front of the upper legs, the back of the lower legs, the ears, the nose, and the face. Long hours riding a bicycle can numb a person to the power of the sun. Use generous amounts of sunscreen and sun block. Treat burns with aloe vera gel. Do not break blisters: You might cause an infection. Keep the affected area clean.

Who Carries the Gear?

The purists of bicycle touring carry all their gear on their bikes in panniers, a set of luggage packs mounted over the wheels. While transporting everything under your own power offers a great feeling of self-sufficiency, the packs make the bike much heavier and harder to maneuver. If you have younger or inexperienced riders, it is wiser and safer to supply a support vehicle (a van or small truck) to carry kids' duffel bags and sleeping bags.

The support vehicle also plays a crucial safety role. It monitors the riding groups by moving along the route in a leapfrog pattern—moving ahead and waiting on the side of the road for groups to pass by. If the vehicle is clearly marked with a sign or an orange flag, it alerts motorists to the presence of bikers on the road and attracts anyone who has helpful information for group leaders. The support vehicle is available to take aboard any biker who is injured or sick. It gives the bike group leaders an immediate response to anyone who needs medical attention for any reason.

Mountain Biking

The widespread availability of mountain bikes opens additional cycling opportunities. The wider width tires provide more stability and confidence on the road. The ruggedness of the frame and tires enables a biker to ride through rough road conditions without having to swerve left into the road or risk falling. Mountain bikes are very appropriate for younger, less experienced riders. As always, helmets should be required on all roads and trails.

Mountain bikes have also opened up new trip possibilities. In many areas, abandoned railroad beds are being renovated into bike paths. Mountain-bike trails offer trip opportunities off the paved road and away from traffic. In addition, many ski areas are now using their trails for mountain biking during the summer. The advantage of such a trip is obvious—no traffic risk. The disadvantage is the distance from civilization when medical help is required. In terms of safety concerns, a mountain-bike trip should be treated like a backpacking trip on wheels, to which we now turn our attention.

Backpacking and Hiking

The storm came over the campsite with incredible speed. The young people were just crawling into their tents for the sleep they so desired after a long strenuous day. Several tents were pitched around the base of a tree.

Suddenly before a drop of rain had fallen, lightning hit the tree. The crack of thunder shook the entire camp. The silence following the thunder was pierced by the hysterical crying of two girls from a tent near the tree.

Al, the youth group leader, had no idea what he would see when he looked inside the tent. One girl lay in her sleeping bag paralyzed. The zipper of the sleeping bag had melted and was permanently welded together. Part of the metal zipper was attached to the skin of this girl's leg. The other girl lay beside her, stunned and unable to hear.

The tent had been pitched within five feet of the tree that was struck by lightning. The roots of the tree extended out from the base and ran directly under the tent. The electrical current had traveled through the roots and into the tent.

One of the volunteer leaders helping with the trip was a surgeon. He assessed the victims' situation and sent a leader for medical help. Fortunately Al and his crew were sleeping overnight near a campground just off the hiking trail. Within an hour the young women were on their way to the hospital.

The girls suffered minor burns from the lightning. The paralysis only lasted for thirty minutes. They were released from the hospital that evening into the care of their parents. Al had called the parents from the hospital. He said it was the most frightening talk he had ever had with a parent on the phone.

The awesome power of natural forces is always on display when a youth group hikes into the wilderness. When the power show becomes too intense, youth workers are often isolated from civilization and professional medical assistance. Al and his group were fortunate to be camped near civilization on that memorable evening. They were thankful to have a trained medical resource with them.

Hiking and backpacking can be very safe, but the smallest problem can become major when medical assistance is hours away. Natural forces and wilderness locations are not to be underestimated as risks for the safety of youth groups.

Hiking and backpacking are not simply camping. If a youth group wants a natural setting with some modern conveniences, a campground is the best choice, for it provides access to transportation and phones. Overnight hiking and backpacking trips that take groups into the wilderness and away from civilization require properly trained leaders.

Before You Hike: Leader Preparation

Before taking a group into the wilderness, the leader has some important work to do:

■ Plan the trip with a high quality map noting any helpful information.

■ Arrange enough leaders to provide a 1-to-3 adult-to-student ratio. (Ten students with three leaders is a maximum number for a wilderness experience.) Don't overlook parents as potential staff leaders. Provide a male staff member to travel with the female staff on all-female trips to discourage aggressive and obnoxious male campers whom they might encounter.

■ Find a trained medical professional (i.e., registered nurse or an emergency medical technician) to travel with you. At the very least, one of your leaders needs extensive first aid training and experience.

■ Take the trip yourself with your team of leaders prior to the group's hike.

■ Talk with the other leaders about the potential dangers of the trip and work through some worst-case scenarios with them.

■ Obtain and distribute information about contacting park rangers and local hospitals.

■ Know the route of the trip so well that you know where and how to find emergency help.

■ Invest in a two-way radio or borrow a cellular phone for the trip, and set up a contacting schedule with your support team. Make several trial runs with the system to make sure you can contact them satisfactorily.

■ Prepare a list of the names of your hikers, complete with medical and insurance information, to carry with you during the trip.

■ Prepare a map and route of your trip plans with a contact person who can alert authorities if you experience difficulties.

■ Pack a fully stocked first aid kit. (See chapter ten for suggestions on contents.)

Ted and several students from his youth group woke up in the mountains of Pennsylvania to find their campsite covered with fresh snow—the product of a surprise spring storm. They weren't prepared for either the knee-deep snow or the windy, cold weather.

They were six miles from yesterday's drop-off spot and a full two-day hike from the spot where their prearranged pick up would be waiting for them. How would they survive these days without suffering frostbite or exposure?

Fortunately Ted and his crew were in the hands of a capable guide they had hired to lead this trip. Two hours of difficult hiking through the snow brought them to a paved road and a waiting van. The guide had responded to the surprise weather conditions by using his portable radio to call his support team and arrange the rendezvous. He explained later that he always has alternate plans ready in case an emergency evacuation is ever needed. What could have been a tragic disaster for Ted and his students was averted by thorough and careful planning.

The Weak Link
■ ■

High-adventure tests the physical and emotional reserves of everyone participating. Sometimes the weakest participant is the adult leader of the youth group.

Physically fit: The leader needs about 150 percent of the energy of the average youth participant. The leader gets the least amount of sleep and expends the most physical and emotional energy dealing with all the problems. Taking a pre-trip with just staff will warn the leader of the physical preparation necessary to build sufficient stamina and will acquaint him or her with the task of removing the uncertainty factors that can drain emotional energy.

Healthy and rested: Leaders often get sick one or two days into a trip because they keep an exhausting schedule just prior to the trip. They are so busy taking care of last-minute details they miss sleep and begin the trip vulnerable to the germs and viruses carried by the students and those present in the trip environment. A sick leader on the second day of the trip destroys the effectiveness of the trip. Plan ahead to get the details done two days prior to the trip departure. Force your leaders to rest and sleep during the days prior to the trip.
■ ■

Student Preparation

Establish some standards of readiness to determine if a student is qualified to participate on a wilderness trip. Students should experience some short, single overnight trips before they are accepted for a multiple-day trip that will take them far from civilization. The short trips will provide a clear picture of their physical fitness and emotional stability necessary for a longer, more challenging trip.

The most crucial piece of equipment on a hiking trip is a good pair of boots or shoes. They must be properly fitted and comfortable to avoid painful and crippling blisters.

Students should wear them regularly prior to the trip.

Any equipment a student is required to furnish should be checked prior to the trip for its quality and reliability. Each student's backpack should be inspected and packed with a staff leader present to ensure that the proper items are included and unnecessary items are left at home. If there is any reason to suspect that students are attempting to smuggle alcohol or drugs on the trip, pack the bag two days prior to the trip. The leader can store the fully packed bag under his or her supervision and release them when they arrive at the drop-off spot.

On the Trail

As you enter the woods and begin to hike the trail, be sure to sign in at the box provided by the forest ranger. This paper is not the place for jokes or phony information. Respect and use this safety procedure. Obey the laws and regulations of the park where you hike. Take time to familiarize your group with the rules and demand everyone's compliance. Other than pocketknives, small axes, and saws, no one should be carrying any type of weapon (such as a firearm or machete).

Never camp:

■ Under tall trees that could attract lightning or whose branches or limbs could fall during a wind storm. Woodsmen call such trees "widow makers."

■ In tall, dry grass. A fire could ignite and spread rapidly to engulf the tents.

■ In a gully or a canyon. A flash flood could start several miles away and rush down, wiping out everything in its path.

■ Near or below the high tide line on a beach or the shoreline.

■ Under an overhanging cliff or bluff. A rock slide or avalanche could bury your campsite.

■ On top of roots of a large, tall tree (remember Al's lesson). Electrical current from lightning hitting the tree can travel through the root system and burn anyone or anything it contacts.

Water purification. This is a necessary task, regardless of the water's source. Your first experience with vomiting and diarrhea caused by impure water will convince you. Purification can be accomplished by three methods: boiling, filtering, or chemical treatment. The chemical treatment is quicker than boiling and more reliable than filtering.

Cleaning dishes and utensils. Campers can come down with diarrhea as a result of dishes that have not been thoroughly cleaned or have not been sufficiently rinsed to remove all soap. Diarrhea is not only inconvenient and uncomfortable; it can trigger severe dehydration.

Food in the camp. Never store food (even the smallest quantities) in the tents where campers are sleeping. Animals of all sizes and types will find a way into that tent perhaps with tragic results. Most obvious is the danger of bears who could do severe damage to any occupant. In bear-free areas, caution still must be taken to discourage common visitors like porcupines and raccoons. A nighttime encounter in close quarters with either of these animals could cause injuries. All food should be placed in a special food bag or backpack and hoisted up on to the limb of a tree where it cannot be reached from the ground or by climbing the tree. Take extra care to ensure that students don't ignore your warning and take snacks to bed with them. The scent of food, even in the crumbs and the opened wrappers, is enough to attract some unwanted visitors.

Fire. Almost every young person loves to build a fire and play with it. The fire must be supervised by a leader at all times. Ignore the pleading of the students and keep the fire small. Build it in an open area (no overhanging trees), in a pit, or inside a ring of rocks to protect it from spreading.

Never use rocks from a lake or stream. They may explode when heated. Make sure the fire is safely away from any tents or tarps. Before you leave the campsite, extinguish the fire completely. Water down any partially burned logs that might ignite after you leave.

Hiking in dense underbrush. Watch for branches and brush swinging into the face and eyes of hikers following the person in front of them. Teach young people how to protect the person who is walking behind them. Never walk on or stand on loose rocks or logs when you can step over or around them. Falling can cause severe sprains or fractures that will seriously alter the outcome of the trip.

Group-mindedness. Hiking and backpacking with a youth group is not an individual experience. Every decision is a group decision. No student should be out of sight of a staff member when on the trail. No one should venture out of the camp area without a partner and giving notice to the leader.

Lost. The group needs prior instruction to know the international distress signal. The SOS signal is three repeated sounds (whistles, etc.) or flashes (flashlight or mirror). The rescue group is to respond with two repeated sounds or flashes. It is good preparation to carry a whistle in your pack at all times. Teach young people to only use the signal in the event of an actual need for help.

Hypothermia. When a person's body becomes unable to generate enough warmth to compensate for heat loss, he or she becomes a victim of hypothermia. It is easier to prevent than to treat. Hypothermia can be prevented by dressing appropriately for the weather, keeping the body and clothing dry, covering the head, neck, and hands, and wearing clothes that maintain insulating properties even when wet. Wet clothing or a cold wind on a body wet with perspiration can lead to hypothermia.

There are two stages of hypothermia. A mildly hypothermic person will complain of cold and have difficulty performing simple motor functions. They may become apathetic, perhaps shivering, and have a body core temperature as low as ninety-five degrees Fahrenheit. Move the person from the cold into a warm environment; then remove damp clothing or add warm insulation. Offer warm liquids and food.

The victim of moderate or severe hypothermia will exhibit slurred speech, stumbling, unresponsiveness, decreased pulse, and breathing difficulty. Body temperature will be below ninety-five F. Cover the victim immediately. Do not allow the person to walk or move. Handle him or her gently. Get medical help. In all situations of potential hypothermia, respond to the signs and symptoms, even if the victim doesn't.

Frostbite. Frostbite is caused by the restriction or stoppage of blood circulation to the extremities such as fingers and toes. The loss of circulation allows the fluid in the tissues to freeze when the surrounding temperature is below thirty-two F. Primary first aid for frostbite involves preventing additional freezing and further damage to the frozen tissue from thawing and refreezing. The main symptom is white skin that is waxy and hard to the touch. The area may feel intensely cold and numb. Give the victim plenty of fluids. Rewarm the part only if it is not going to bear weight and will not refreeze. Do not rub or massage the area. Take the person to a hospital.

Insect bites and stings. Unless the victim suffers an allergic reaction, bites and stings are usually more painful than serious. For bee stings use a knife edge to scrape out the stinger. Using tweezers or grabbing the stinger with fingernails may squeeze more venom in the sting area. Wash with soap and apply a anti-sting lotion. If the victim suffers an allergic reaction, give him or her an antihistamine, keep calm, maintain the airway, and transport the person to a hospital. People who know they are allergic should carry an Ana-Kit that contains a premeasured injection to fight the reaction.

Poison oak, poison ivy, and poison sumac. Learn to identify poisonous plants. Poison oak and poison ivy both go by the rule "leaves of three, let them be." The plants secrete a noxious oil that severely irritates the skin when transmitted by direct contact and contact with contaminated clothing. Signs appear within one or two days after contact: skin burns, itches, and sometimes blisters. If you suspect contact with such plants, remove the contaminated clothes and wash separately. Wash the skin with strong laundry soap and warm (not hot) water. Wipe down the affected area with rubbing alcohol. If rash develops, avoid scratching, for it could lead to a secondary infection if the blisters are opened. Apply cold compresses and a lotion containing hydrocortisone.

Rock Climbing and Rappelling

If you can't hire or recruit a certified experienced instructor, you and your youth group shouldn't even attempt rock climbing or rappelling. Most insurance companies will no longer cover these activities. Check your insurance policy.

If you go looking for a guide, ask about his or her training (National Outdoor Leadership School [NOLS] is probably the best) and the experience he or she has had leading groups. Check the references; don't take any shortcuts. The lives of your students will be in their hands. Be sure to take the staff on a pretrip experience with the guide to get a clear understanding of what is involved.

Despite the best training and equipment, rock climbing and rappelling accidents do happen. Recently a youth organization suffered a fatality when the professional guide did not tie the rope to the harness correctly. It was something he had done successfully thousands of times prior. In this type of activity, a small, rare mistake can mean severe injury or death.

On the Witness Stand
■ ■ ■ ■ ■ ■ ■ ■ ■ ■ ■ ■ ■ ■ ■ ■ ■ ■ ■

I can still hear Chrissy screaming. She was thirty feet below me, literally hanging on a rope by her hair. Chrissy was one of fifteen students who had accepted the challenge from me and one of my volunteers to rappel down a seventy-foot cliff. Charlie made his living as an arborist (tree trimmer) and climbed with ropes regularly. He had the equipment, the know-how, and the persuasiveness to talk me into offering this adventure to the kids at our YFC camp.

It had been a great afternoon until Chrissy's long hair came out of her bandanna and became entwined in the rope. She was not wearing any protective headgear (a major blunder on my part). When her hair caught in the rope, she panicked and abandoned her rappelling handgrip position to grab the rope any way she could and keep her hair from being pulled out of her head.

Charlie heard the scream and jumped over the edge Indiana Jones-style, grabbing an adjacent rope on the way down. It was extremely reckless, but effective. He reached Chrissy, stabilized her position, and cut her hair from the rope with his hunting knife. Slowly he lowered himself (Chrissy clung to him with a death hold) to safety.

We laughed and bragged about the whole incident later that night at our camp. It did give me a great opportunity to talk to Chrissy (a noted agnostic) about who she was praying to while hanging on the rope. But I was a stupid, foolish leader who just dodged a major bullet. Except for Charlie's heroic reaction, Chrissy had been seconds from a major injury or death.

In a court of law, I would have been asked about Charlie's credentials and training to lead such an activity. Why didn't we use protective headgear? Why didn't her parents know when she went to camp with us she would be rappelling down a seventy-foot cliff? The questions would be endless. The conclusion would be clear. I foolishly miscalculated the risk and allowed Chrissy to be in the situation that threatened her life.
■ ■ ■ ■ ■ ■ ■ ■ ■ ■ ■ ■ ■ ■ ■ ■ ■ ■ ■ ■

NINE

Most Accidents
Happen at Home

It was Friday night and time for Death Tag! With all the lights off in the church, the students hid throughout the building. The youth director searched for them, armed with butterscotch candies that he threw at them to "kill" them. In a past game, one student hid in the rafters above a false ceiling. During the game he slipped off the rafters and crashed through the ceiling to the floor. This night a young man fleeing through the basement ran into a water pipe and burst the pipe. Try explaining that to a trustee of the church.

Most of us in youth ministry acknowledge the need for safety when we are climbing a mountain or canoeing on a white-water river. When the setting changes to our church building and our regular weekly meetings, we feel much more relaxed and complacent on safety issues. The scenery is so familiar that we are blinded to the hazards and risks. Like the mature, experienced water-ski instructor who broke his own safety rules (see chapter seven), our familiarity with normal youth group activities breeds contempt for awareness of danger.

In chapter two we surveyed a church facility open for an evening of unstructured recreation and listed the potential dangerous situations. Most of us have learned to feel comfortable with how our youth ministry operates. It may look potentially hazardous to a newcomer, but we have adjusted our nerves to accept the risk. Most likely we have done these activities numerous times and operated with our loose rules without any serious injuries or problems.

The warning of this book calls youth leaders to recognize a changing culture that will examine and evaluate their activities and safety practices with greater scrutiny. What may have been quickly forgiven in the past may be cause for a lawsuit in the present and coming days.

Facility Hazards

Safety agencies tell us most accidents happen at home. If that is true, the regular meeting place of our youth group is the "home" location we should be safety-proofing. Often it is so familiar to us that we cannot see the hazards right in front of us each week.

■ Are there smoke detectors and fire extinguishers in the building? Are the extinguishers hidden to keep our youth group kids from fooling with them? Without looking, do you know where they are? Is there fire emergency equipment in the kitchen?

■ Are emergency phone numbers posted in a public place near the phone? Is there a phone to use in an emergency, or are they all behind locked doors?

■ What access do our students have to balconies and high places in the church or building? Can they get onto the roof or out on the fire escape? Falls are a common reason for serious accidents and injuries.

■ Is the recreation room or gym equipped with safety equipment such as protective mats at the ends of the basketball court?

■ Is there a well-stocked first aid kit available?

Eyes on the Equipment

The greatest risk of danger with equipment isn't when the whole group is using it, but rather when it sits unsupervised. A careful youth leader keeps equipment and props under careful control and put away when not being used properly.

In chapter six, I recounted the story of a youth ministry

volunteer who was paralyzed by falling off the top of the cage ball at a field event. Just days ago, I was at a youth event where a six-foot cage ball was used for a great junior high game. Later in the evening, while most everyone was in an adjacent room eating snacks, I walked into the game room to discover an eighth-grader who had hopped on top of the ball and was starting to walk on it, to the amazement of his two watching friends. I spoke softly and calmly so I wouldn't frighten him into falling. When he was safely on the ground and out the door, I shook my head in disbelief at how easy it is to leave temptation in the way of students.

One youth group leader hooked up a rope swing from the cathedral ceiling in the youth room meeting area. He had one of the volunteer leaders swing on the rope as part of a skit they did for the kids in the meeting. After the meeting the rope was still hanging from the ceiling hook, but it was not attached securely. A young man tried to mimic what he had seen the leader do during the meeting. He grabbed the rope, swung off the ten-foot ledge, and immediately crashed to the floor. It was a big surprise for him. Fortunately he walked away with just some bruises.

Teenage Vehicles

This is a hot home safety issue. Youth leaders can't control what teenagers drive to their meetings. You probably have cars, trucks, motorcycles, mopeds, and bicycles of many types in your parking lot. That parking lot can be a dangerous spot for your kids.

Teenagers have always been able to find something exciting (and dangerous) to do with motorized vehicles. Last summer one group had a lot of fun "surfing the hood" of the cars. Several students would stand on the front hood of the car, surfer-style, as the driver whipped around the parking lot. The driver would accelerate and brake, trying to make the surfers lose their balance. Our family was asked to pray for one young man who was in a coma after he lost his footing on the hood and hit his head on the pavement.

A youth leader can't wipe out the fascination teenagers have with motorized vehicles. These games will come and go. But in the course of these games, students will be hurt. Our responsibility is to monitor what goes on when they are under our supervision and demand their best behavior and safe operation of those vehicles. For more on this subject see the discussion of teenage drivers in chapter five.

Dangerous Games

Food games. Campus Life calls it Chubby Bunnies. You may have a different name for it. You get a student to fill his or her mouth with marshmallows, grapes, etc., one at a time, while repeating a phrase like "chubby bunnies." Several students are in competition to see who can have the most items in their mouths while still being able to repeat the phrase. It is very funny to hear students slurring their responses while slobbery food drips out of their mouths. Can you recognize the danger? Gasping for breath, a piece of food could be drawn into their windpipes, causing them to choke.

This game practically begs you to perform the Heimlich maneuver on a participant. I can hear the groaning from my YFC friends: "But it is so funny...I've never seen anyone choke." I hear your objections, but think about it. Is it worth the risk? The comic value of the game would be lost in a courtroom when you are asked to explain the purpose of the game.

We should give special scrutiny to any forced-feeding game that puts large amounts of food in a person's mouth. Dropping food into the mouth of a person lying on the floor or shooting food into a person's mouth is also not a good idea because of the risk of choking. We used to hold pizza eating contests, where guys would eat a triangular slice in less than ten seconds. It can't be healthy or safe for young people to ingest large amounts of food without chewing. Should we as leaders be encouraging the game and challenging them to go faster?

Move the furniture, Fred. Lack of foresight and preparation can put a dent in the head of a student. If you conduct a game in a living room setting, be sure to allow adequate space for a person to fall, or place spotters around the room so students cannot fall.

A young man fainted during a game in a family room. He was blowing on one end of a clear plastic tube trying to force a raw egg (in the middle of the tube) into the mouth of the student who was blowing into the other end. When his breath was exhausted, he fainted and fell backward into the corner of a table. The impact split open his head. It meant a trip to the emergency room and stitches to close the wound.

A young lady was placed in the center of the circle for a game called Pass the Bod. She was instructed to stand stiff while the other students sat in a circle around her with their stocking feet against her legs. When she crossed her arms in front of her chest she was to lean toward the group. The students on the floor were supposed to push and pass her around the group. Usually this game is a blast, but on this night when the young lady was pushed toward the other side of the circle, the students didn't catch her. She landed face first on the edge of a wooden end table, knocking out her two front teeth.

In both of these accidents, the leaders had not provided spotters to guard the participants if they should fall. Pass the Bod needs several reliable spotters around the circle. The games were played in inappropriate settings. The close proximity of the furniture reflects a lack of planning and anticipation of what could happen when people fall. Games need to be selected according to the physical setting of the meeting room.

Throwing games. Throwing any objects in a youth group meeting needs to be carefully monitored. Throwing activities need to be defined with a safe target, specific objects to be thrown, and a clear starting and stopping point. If a "throwing" atmosphere develops in the meeting, you can expect anything and everything to be thrown—paper wads, pencils, or wrapped candy. Some of the objects will be absolutely harmless. Others can be dangerous. You can't expect young people to always know the difference and to exercise good judgment.

Hitting games. Who defines how hard students are supposed to hit a person in the head with a newspaper during a game? Most students may hit gently and harmlessly. A student, frustrated or excited about the game, might forget his strength and blast a younger, smaller group member in the head or face. Some students easily lose control when they are struck by someone with whom they might feel some competition. They might lose control and get out of hand to go one-up on someone else in the group.

Beware the eyes. Spraying anything in the eyes and face of a young person is strictly taboo. You might damage the eyes or a person's glasses or contact lenses. Sharp objects should not be used in games where a sudden unexpected movement might cause someone to strike a person's eye. Watch for blindfold games where a person might unknowingly strike another person's eyes. I certainly felt different about my Cops and Robbers game (see chapter six) when six hands started pawing my face and eyes trying to pull a piece of tape off my face.

No weapons. We used to stage a fake assassination in youth group meetings to shock everyone and set the stage for discussing violence. A stranger (arranged by our staff) would walk into the meeting and fire a starter pistol. A staff leader would be "struck" Hollywood-style and fall to the ground bleeding as the stranger escaped. Although it was dramatic, that was probably not one of our better discussion starters. It was simply a stunt that pumped the emotions of kids. Today I would never do any stunt involving weapons in my meetings. Some young person sitting in the meeting might pull out a real weapon to avenge what he just witnessed without knowing it was just an act.

Hide-and-Seek games. Youth leaders interviewed for this book told numerous stories about young people (and leaders) hurt during Hide-and-Seek games in their church buildings. These games encourage students to find remote and unlikely places in a building to hide. Students have gotten stuck in crawl spaces and fallen through ceilings. One young man fell through the ceiling into a storage room off the sanctuary and just missed being impaled on the large metal candelabra (used for weddings) being stored there.

Scaring kids. Manny was new to the youth group. He liked coming with his friends. Everyone seemed to like him. One night the group set up a funny game where after spending a few minutes in the dark, a person would be blasted with a bright strobe light and see himself in a mirror. The game really worked well on Manny. When the light flashed and he saw a face right in front of him, he reacted spontaneously and punched the mirror, cutting his hand. If you decide to scare teenagers, be ready for a physical reaction or response. Don't have anything or anyone within reach that could cause injury. Manny's family sued the church and was awarded $25,000 in damages.

Rough games. Without protection, heavy contact games in the church gym or the yard outside are an unnecessary risk to the safety of the young people involved. Many youth groups love to have a friendly game of tackle football (leaders included). Neck, head, and dental injuries are the major risks. These injuries are much harder to repair than bruises or even broken bones. The most likely scenario for injury is when young people of varying physical sizes and abilities are in the same game. The weaker and less skilled are at high risk when they have no protection.

Sports plus. When Terry showed up with a mini-trampoline, everyone in the church gym lined up for the slam dunk contest. During the first night a staff leader wrecked his knee. Terry missed in his attempt to swing on the rim after his dunk and fell to the floor breaking both of his arms. With spotters and some supervision, sports activities like this can be within the safety guidelines. Terry and his leader didn't take time to think about making it safe.

Outdoor field games. For a full listing on camps and retreats, see chapter six.

Dangerous Topics

Suicide. A youth group meeting led by a young inexperienced staff leader tackled the topic of suicide. Someone asked if a person who was a Christian would go to heaven if he or she committed suicide. The discussion focused on how heaven would be so great because all the problems of life on earth would be forgotten. None of the leaders wanted to say that suicide victims go to hell because some of the students had a friend who had taken his life.

Several young people with many problems and struggles went home that night with the thought that the sooner they could get to heaven, the better it would be for them. During that week one of them made an unsuccessful suicide attempt.

A suicide discussion can provoke an interest in the exact behavior you are trying to condemn (the same is true for discussions of the occult). It should never be scheduled into the meeting calendar routinely or handled casually. If it is necessary to discuss suicide, be sure to present a clear message that it is never a good answer to any problem a person is facing. Be alert to any young person who indicates any interest in the subject or is facing pressure or depression. Give him or her personal attention and follow up with further discussion immediately after the meeting, within twenty-four hours, and throughout the week.

Sexual or physical abuse. These topics are very hot and loaded with deep emotion. Extreme care must be taken not to trivialize the way you handle these matters. The chances are good that someone in your group has been abused. The youth leader should seek help to handle this subject carefully.

The safety factor is the liability leaders carry if they learn about abuse in the lives of students. This information should be handled with complete confidentiality in the context of the youth group. It will hurt young people to have a staff leader discuss confidential information with any other student. Information on reporting abuse can be found later in this chapter.

Sex. Today's youth culture is dominated by sexual topics and information. Josh McDowell's "Why Wait?" campaign reports that church teenagers are engaging in sexual activity at a rate similar to the general teenage population—approximately 60 percent. When sexuality is discussed in your youth ministry, leaders need to be very careful. In a large group setting, both male and female staff can interact with the whole group. Small group discussions or one-to-one counseling, though, should be conducted strictly by the same-gender staff leader. It is extremely dangerous and totally inappropriate for male leaders to be counseling teenage girls about their sexuality. The same principle applies to female staff and teenage boys.

Special Events

When you travel with your group to a one-night special event, think about how their safety can be protected. Transportation is a key issue. Have your staff prepared with information and directions so that no one gets lost or separated from the group. Don't let the excitement of arriving at your special destination cause the group to ignore simple safety practices like crossing the street in traffic. The daughter of a youth leader was running from a youth event to the church bus without regard to the traffic on the street. She was struck by a car and killed.

Beware of events with a general admission policy (no reserved seats). If there is a wait for the doors to open, the crowd can develop an aggressive attitude about getting the best seats. Pushing and shoving can lead to a mob scene when the doors open. It is illegal in many cities to have large events in concert hall/stadium settings with just general admission tickets. Don't allow your students to run into the hall to get their seats. If they fall, they could be trampled and seriously hurt. If you find yourself in a potentially dangerous situation at a concert or special event, don't be afraid to voice your concern to security guards or people in charge. You can speak up to the groups around you and ask for calm for the safety of everyone. If necessary, pull your group off to the side of the crowd until the situation is less dangerous.

Give specific instructions to your students about the conduct you expect from them at a concert or special event. Be sure they know their boundaries, where to find you, where and when to meet for departure, and not to leave the facility for any reason. Work out a procedure with your staff to check up on all your students during the evening. You don't need any surprises at the end of the night.

When you return to the church or your pickup point, an adult should remain there until all the students have been picked up by parents or designated drivers. Try to stick to the arrival and departure times you set for parents. Have a phone chain set of parents whom you can call if you are going to be more than thirty minutes late. If you are taking students home and are delayed, stop to have the students call home. A worried, angry parent is tough to handle late at night. If the youth ministry staff is taking everyone home, have the drivers confirm with you that everyone is home safely. Those short phone calls are a perfect time for you to say thanks for their help, while sending a message of concern for every young person and his or her family.

Discipline Problems

In the ideal world, youth group students listen to the leaders and carefully follow all their instructions. But do I need to remind you that we live in a fallen world? We all have days when our students seem uncontrollable and deaf to our guidance.

Young people running out of control are like an infectious disease in the atmosphere of the group. This attitude threatens the safety and well-being of everyone involved. The youth leader needs to stop any out-of-control actions immediately before the problem spreads. Picture a table of students and leaders in a camp dining room. If two people at a single table start throwing food at each other, how long does it take to get other students and tables involved and throwing food. The responsible leader must never be afraid to step into any situation like that and gently but firmly remind the young people of the safety standards and who ultimately is in charge of the youth program.

Sometimes it is just silliness getting out of hand. I remember a fall weekend retreat when squirt guns advanced to cups of water that progressed to bowls, pitchers, and buckets of water.

I was in the kitchen working with the students who were on dishwashing duty. I was angered when some of them left their posts to join the water mania. I was also angered by the mess they made spilling water all over the kitchen floor.

When I had reached my boiling point, I grabbed one of the little guys who had hijacked the kitchen faucet and forcefully picked him up and threw him out the door onto the steps of the building. Everyone else got the message and scattered for cover. I physically hurt this young man. I was mad and had lost my temper. I had to publicly apologize to the whole group later that evening.

Youth leaders must not hit, punch, fight, or in any way physically abuse any student. It may prompt a legal action against you. Verbal abuse may be just as bad. Calling names and using sarcasm may win the initial battle, but these actions undermine the long-term ministry you will have with any group or individual.

When you are facing a young person who is physically acting out, hurting you or others, you must restrain him or her to protect the safety of others in the group. However the force of the youth leader must be defensive and restrained. Youth leaders can obtain special training in passive resistance, a satisfactory way of calming a person who is out of control. Check with a secular health and human service agency in your area for additional information on such training.

Safety Issues and Discipline

Are students leaving your meetings and activities early or disappearing for periods of time during the meeting? You can't erect a wall around your youth program to keep kids in, but you do have an obligation to the parents. Response to this behavior is somewhat related to the age of the young people, but anyone in junior high school or high school is still under the authority and supervision of his or her parent/guardian. If the parents think the kids are attending the youth group, the youth leader must tell them if in fact those kids are not.

When a young person exits early, the youth leader should confront that person directly and let him or her know the action is unacceptable. The leader should also outline the obligation he or she has to the parents. If the student continues to cut out, the youth leader must inform the parents and work together to change the behavior.

Drug Problems

How would you handle a strong suspicion by one of your volunteer leaders that a young person who is attending your group regularly is selling drugs to other youth in your group? What is your safety responsibility when you are providing the social meeting place for these transactions? Experience has taught me you can't turn your head and think the problem will go away. However, you shouldn't jump to conclusions and condemn the suspected person without a thorough investigation.

If kids want to sell and buy drugs, it is almost impossible for you to stop them from doing so, on or off your turf. However, you can take action. Confront kids suspected of being involved as sellers or buyers. They may lie to your face, but you can send a strong message about how you are going to fight the sale and use of drugs in the youth program. You can let them know that they will be under your watchful eye. Explain that you will personally confront them and bring other significant people (like their parents) into the matter if you have any evidence of their involvement. Then keep your promises. It's another way to show you care.

Have you decided what your response will be to students who show up to your meetings or activities showing signs of drinking or drug use? Will you let them stay and sit quietly in the meeting or will you ask them to leave? The youth ministry team needs to make that decision prior to the incident. If you do decide to let them stay, what special precautions will the youth ministry staff make to keep them from disrupting the meeting or hurting others?

The youth leader should not be handling these matters alone. Although it may seem embarrassing or condemning to your leadership, share these issues with your superior and/or board leaders. Don't let them be surprised about a drug problem in their ministry when some bad news becomes public. Ask for their help and guidance. They share the responsibility with you. When it is appropriate, talk to parents individually. They should not be left uninformed about major struggles in the life of their young person. Your pastor or director can be of great help to you as you relate to the parents.

Reporting Sexual Abuse and Physical Abuse

All suspicions of sexual abuse or physical abuse must be reported by volunteer workers to the head of the youth ministry. The head of the youth ministry should discuss these reports immediately with the director or pastor of the organization.

All this should be done quickly and confidentially.

In many states the professional youth worker or pastor has been designated a mandated reporter who must report any allegations of abuse to a hot line run by the state government.

Check the regulations of your state and comply with them. Often there is a mandated time period (twenty-four to forty-eight hours) in which youth workers must report what they have learned. Learn the process and system in your state.

The first time I called the sexual abuse hot line, I agonized over my decision. One of our female volunteers had been told by a sixteen-year-old girl that her stepfather was coming into her room at night and sexually touching her. When the volunteer told me, I was shocked. This was an active church family. Everything about this family looked great on the outside.

We sent one of our female staff workers with the volunteer to talk with the girl to confirm what she had said. The staff worker then reported the girl's allegations to me. As the director of the program, I knew the law required me to make the call. I was afraid of what would happen to everyone involved and how the state agency would respond. I knew my call would set off a chain reaction that would forever alter the lives of these people.

I called the sexual abuse hot line. I was impressed with how much care and time the state agency took with my report and my concerns about the family. I realize that state agencies mishandle some situations and that the quality of the response depends on the person assigned to the case, but I found some good people waiting at the other end of the line to help. They responded immediately, contacting the young woman at school and the parents when they arrived home from work. The mother admitted that she had suspicions but had been afraid to confront her spouse. The stepfather agreed to undergo counseling. The young woman was taken out of the home and placed with her grandmother several miles away.

There are still many issues facing each person in that family, but our action brought about significant positive change in that young woman's life. She hated us for a few weeks after we reported it. That was hard on all of us, especially the volunteer whom she initially told. Several months later, though, she was grateful that we had acted and that she was not being abused anymore.

Inappropriate Staff Relationships

One of the crucial safety issues of ministry each week from your home base is the relationship the youth ministry staff have with the young people in the program. In chapter four, I discussed the standards for sexual conduct for youth ministry staff (paid and volunteer). These standards must be more than a piece of paper, signed and placed in a file. They must be followed each week by the staff and monitored regularly by the leader.

The story of Steve, a volunteer staff guy who had been accused of rape by a girl in the club (see chapter four), reminds us that youth ministry today requires special precautions. Allegations of sexual misconduct in a youth ministry will destroy the credibility of God's work in that community. Special attention must be paid to the habits and practices of staff so that no actual misconduct can begin to grow or be alleged against any youth ministry staff person.

There should not be even the hint of any romantic or sexual attraction between staff and young people. Staff must be alert not to transmit any verbal or nonverbal messages that would suggest it. Dating or going out with any high school student should be absolutely forbidden to youth ministry staff and volunteers. Staff should use the buddy system (having another staff present or outside hearing distance but clearly visible) when talking privately or counseling a student of the opposite sex. Driving alone with students of the opposite sex should be avoided. Physical contact (touching, hugging, kissing, massaging, etc.) that might be interpreted as romantic or sexual should be prohibited between staff and students. Staff members who seem to focus on one or two kids as favorites must be counseled to widen their approach or face dismissal from the ministry.

Any suspicions of misconduct or signs of romantic interests should be voiced and confronted immediately. Put a watch on people who continue to walk too close to the line. Those who have impure motives are often skilled at hiding the truth. Don't be naive or uninformed. Be active in maintaining upstanding relationships with all your students. Anyone who refuses to comply with your standards or who violates your written guidelines should be brought before your supervisor to discuss how changes will be made or how the person will be released from the youth ministry team.

TEN

Dealing With Problems and Injuries

■■■■■■■■■■■■■■■■■■■■■■■

As I reached the crest of the hill, I saw bikers standing in the road three hundred yards ahead. Someone was lying along the edge of the road. I covered the distance in record time and jumped off my bike looking for the group's leader. The teenagers stood motionless like frozen statues. The screams came from our leader who was lying face down on the pavement in a growing pool of blood.

Disclaimer
■■■■■■■■■■■■■■■■■■■■■■■

The following information does not substitute for certified first aid training that should be required of all youth ministry staff. This section should not be regarded as a replacement for seeking immediate assistance from a trained medical professional or a medical facility.

This information is designed only to alert youth leaders to common problems and first aid techniques that they should learn from a qualified trainer or organization. This information does not constitute training in first aid. Every youth ministry should have staff trained in first aid at all activities.

■■■■■■■■■■■■■■■■■■■■■■

Stacy was a summer volunteer on our bike trip staff. She had gotten too much sun on the first day out of Montreal. This was her first day back on the bike after four days in the support van. I would learn later that she was riding really tight on the back wheel of the lead biker to conserve her strength. She touched that back tire and hit a rut in the road launching her over the handlebars. Her face skidded to

■ ■

Much of the information in this chapter is drawn from the first aid and safety manuals published by the American Red Cross. Their manuals provide extensive and complete information on first aid response in much greater detail than this chapter. Reading this chapter should motivate every youth worker to register with the American Red Cross or a similar organization for first aid training.

■ ■

a stop on the pavement.

Her screams signaled that she was conscious and breathing. I barked out orders for two students to get to a phone at a house across the road. I described our location as they turned to run. Stacy began to cough and choke. She lifted her face from the pavement. I checked her airway. Surprisingly her teeth looked intact. As with any injury to the mouth or nose, the blood was flowing profusely. I called for the first aid kit and the gauze compresses to slow down the bleeding. There were more cuts on her body than we had pads of gauze.

Inside I was terrified. This was way over my head and the minimal first aid training I had completed. I prayed and worried at the same time. What was I going to do if she lost consciousness or started having convulsions? We were ten miles outside of the nearest town. How long would it take the ambulance to find us?

My prayers were answered when a woman stepped out of a car and announced she was an emergency room nurse. She pulled a sleeping bag out of her trunk to keep Stacy warm. Until the ambulance arrived, she worked like an angel sent to help us.

It took seventy-three stitches to close the gashes in Stacy's face. Three months later you couldn't have guessed she had been lying on the side of that road. Though her scars disappeared quickly, my feeling of inadequate preparation for a medical emergency stayed with me. Everyone I know in youth ministry has a deep desire to help people who are in need. Each of us can learn how to respond to physical needs in these moments of emergency if we will take time to be trained and prepared.

First Aid

Administering first aid is often just a matter of common sense. The primary task is to remain calm, assess the situation, call for help, provide comfort, and tend to the needs of the injured person as best you are able until help arrives. The basic principle of first aid is to do good if you can, while being careful not to do any harm.

Three Actions to Take in Any Emergency
1. Check the scene and the victim(s)
2. Call 911 or your local emergency number
3. Care for the victim(s)

Basic Steps of First Aid

1. Upon seeing the injured person, assess the situation for any additional possibility of injury to anyone else (including yourself). Make sure no one else will be injured. Would you be in danger if you tried to approach the victim to administer first aid? Don't put yourself in danger.

2. Do not move the injured person unless he or she is in an immediate, life-threatening situation. Anytime an injured person is moved, there is risk of additional injury that might cause permanent damage or death. If you have to move the victim, do it as quickly and carefully as possible. Avoid twisting or bending the victim, who might have a neck or spine injury.

3. Call 911 or the local emergency number. If possible send another person present to make the call.

When You Know You Should Call 911

When the person
- is or becomes unconscious.
- has trouble breathing.
- has chest pain or pressure.
- is bleeding severely.
- has pain or pressure in the abdomen that does not go away.
- is vomiting or passing blood.
- has seizures, a severe headache, or slurred speech.
- appears to have been poisoned.
- has injuries to the head, neck, or back.
- has possible broken bones.

Calling 911: What to Tell Them

Tell the dispatcher
- the exact location or address of the emergency.
- the telephone number from where you are calling.
- your name.
- what happened to injure the victim.
- how many people are involved.
- the condition of the victim(s).
- what first aid is being administered.

Do not hang up until the dispatcher hangs up. He or she may need more information or may instruct you on how to care for the victim. Return to care for the victim until the ambulance arrives. If you send someone else to call, be sure that he or she knows the answers to these questions. Remind the caller not to hang up before the dispatcher does.

4. Begin caring for the victim. Always care for life-threatening situations before those that are not life-threatening. Watch for changes in the victim's breathing and consciousness. Keep the person warm. Help the victim rest comfortably. Calm and comfort the victim.

5. If the victim is unconscious, you should check three signs:

■ Is the victim breathing? If not, you have a life-threatening situation. Check by putting your face close to the person's mouth and nose. Watch to see if his or her chest rises or falls. Check the airways for blockage. If there is no breathing, you must give the victim a couple breaths.

■ Does the victim have a pulse? Place your finger on the front of the person's neck in the groove next to the Adam's apple. If there is a pulse but the person is not breathing, you will have to do rescue breathing. If there is no pulse, you will have to do CPR. At that moment you will be glad you sought training from the Red Cross or other organization. Don't wait until you are in this situation to recognize your need for training.

■ Is the victim bleeding severely? Check the victim's body from head to toe for signs of bleeding. Bleeding is severe when blood spurts out of a wound. Control the bleeding by placing a clean covering such as a sterile dressing over the wound and applying pressure. A dressing can be any clean cloth or absorbent material (clothing, bandanna, or sanitary napkin). Add additional dressings to the wound while maintaining constant pressure until the bleeding is controlled.

6. If the victim is conscious, ask him or her what happened. A verbal response confirms the victim's breathing and pulse. Look for any other life-threatening conditions. Talk to the victim or any witnesses to determine what care you need to give. Check the person for any problems. Don't move the victim or ask him or her to move. Watch for changes in breathing and consciousness. Look for a medical alert tag on

the neck or wrist. If the injury or illness is related to the person's condition, call the number listed for help.

7. Stabilize any fractures or dislocations to prevent any further discomfort or harm. Any setting of a fracture or dislocation must be done by a trained medical professional.

8. Always treat for shock. Shock is a life-threatening condition even if the injury is not. Shock can be brought on by injury, poisoning, illness, allergic reaction, and even by seeing someone else injured. The signs and symptoms of shock are weakness, pale color, cool and clammy skin, irregular breathing, nausea, dizziness, and shivering. The first task is to maintain the injured person's body temperature by wrapping him or her in an emergency blanket, sleeping bag, or extra clothing if the outside temperature is cold. If the temperature is hot, keep the person cool by creating shade. Always try to keep the person insulated from the ground. The general rule is to keep the injured person lying down, comfortable and resting with the feet raised (except in case of head, neck, or back injury or if you suspect broken bones). Control any external bleeding. Calm and reassure the victim. Although the person is likely to be thirsty, don't give him or her anything to eat or drink. If the injured person feels like moving or sitting up, don't restrain him or her.

9. If the person has a partially blocked airway and is coughing forcefully, let him or her try to cough up the object. A person who can cough is getting enough air to breath. Stay with him and encourage him to keep coughing. If the victim can't dislodge the object, call an ambulance.

A person whose airway is completely blocked will not be able to speak, cough forcefully, or breathe. The victim may cough weakly or make high-pitched noises. Have a bystander call an ambulance while you begin care. To open the airway quickly, give a series of quick hard thrusts to the victim's abdomen. Acquaint yourself thoroughly with the Heimlich maneuver.

Dealing With Common Injuries

Open wounds (cuts and lacerations). The best treatment is cleansing the wound with antibacterial soap and water. Apply a clean, nonstick dressing and secure it with adhesive tape. For serious bleeding, apply direct pressure immediately using a clean dressing. If you don't think the wound also involves a broken bone, elevate the wound above the heart to slow the bleeding. When the bleeding stops, secure the wound with a compression bandage, and travel to the hospital for additional treatment. If the bleeding cannot be controlled, put pressure on the nearby artery (pressure point). Treat for shock. It is brought on by a loss of blood or a disruption in the circulation system. Infection is a major concern for all wounds. Always clean with soap and water before applying an antibacterial ointment to prevent infection. After you have completed caring for the victim, be sure to wash your hands immediately.

Severe wounds. If a part of the body has been severed or torn off, try to find the part and wrap it in sterile gauze or any clean material. Put the wrapped part in a plastic bag. Keep it cool with ice, but do not freeze it. Take it to the hospital with the victim. Doctors may be able to reattach it.

If an object is impaled in the wound of a victim, do not try to remove it. Place several dressings around it to keep it from moving. Bandage the dressings in place around the object.

Wounds that break through the abdomen can cause the organs to push out. Carefully remove clothing from around the wound. Cover the organs with a moist, sterile or clean dressing and cover it with plastic wrap. Place a folded towel or other cloth over the dressing to keep the organs warm.

Dental. If the victim has had a tooth knocked out or damaged, place a sterile dressing directly in the space now vacant or damaged. Tell the victim to bite down carefully. If you can recover the tooth, it is important to get it replanted in the socket within an hour. Handle the knocked out tooth with care, picking it up by the chewing edge (crown) not the root. Do not touch the root part of the tooth. If possible place the tooth back into the socket. Bite down gently and hold the tooth in place with a sterile dressing. If it can't be placed back in the socket, place it in a container of cool, fresh milk until you reach the dentist. If no milk is available, use water.

Eyes. If any chemical or debris gets in a person's eye, flush the eye with large amounts of water. Be sure to flush from the inside corner of the eye (nearest to the bridge of the nose) outward so the other eye is not also contaminated. Continue to flush the eye for ten to fifteen minutes until you are sure the chemical or debris has been removed. Remove any thickened substance from the eye with a clean, moist cloth. Flush the eye again. Do not put any medications in the eye. Cover the injured eye with a sterile gauze pad and take the person to the hospital immediately.

Burns. Minor burns usually don't require medical attention. Treatment, however, should be taken seriously. The affected part should be immersed in cool water to reduce pain and stop the burning sensation. Clean the area with soap and water and apply a topical anesthetic to reduce pain. For more severe burns that blister or have deep tissue damage, the victim needs immediate medical attention.

Don't apply ice directly to any burn unless it is very minor. Don't touch a burn with anything except a clean covering. Don't remove pieces of cloth that stick to the burned area. Don't try to clean a severe burn. Don't break blisters or use any kind of ointment on a severe burn.

Sprains. Falls or hits that suddenly twist a joint can cause sprains to wrists, knees, and ankles. It is almost impossible to distinguish between a break and a sprain without an X-ray. You should assume that the limb is broken, then elevate it and immobilize it. Apply a cold pack to minimize swelling until the injured person can be examined at the hospital.

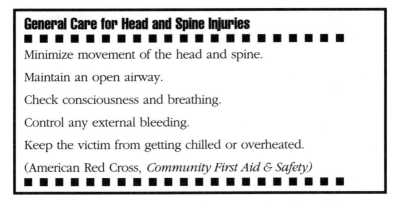

General Care for Head and Spine Injuries

Minimize movement of the head and spine.

Maintain an open airway.

Check consciousness and breathing.

Control any external bleeding.

Keep the victim from getting chilled or overheated.

(American Red Cross, *Community First Aid & Safety*)

Spinal injuries. Signs of spinal injury include a change in consciousness, problems with breathing and vision, inability to move a body part, an ongoing headache, nausea, vomiting, and loss of balance. When you recognize these signs, call an ambulance at once. While you wait for assistance, give care by helping the victim minimize any movement of his or her head or spine. Place your hands on both sides of the victim's head. Position the head gently in line with the body and support it in that position until medical personnel arrive. If you feel resistance or it hurts the victim as you try to do this, stop. Support the head as you found it.

Seizures. These may range from mild blackouts that

could be mistaken for daydreaming to sudden uncontrolled muscular contractions lasting several minutes. Stay calm, knowing that most seizures last only a few minutes. Have someone call for an ambulance. Protect the person from injury and keep his or her airway clear. Don't put anything in the person's mouth, though, especially your fingers. If there is fluid, saliva, blood, or vomit in their mouth, roll the person over on one side to drain it and keep the airway open.

Fainting. This is a temporary loss of consciousness. It is often preceded by paleness and perspiring. To care for fainting, place the victim on his or her back, elevate the feet and loosen any restrictive clothing. Although fainting victims recover quickly with no lasting effects, the symptom may actually be a signal of a more serious condition.

Asthma attacks. Asthma is a condition that narrows the air passages and makes breathing very difficult. The asthma victim makes wheezing noises when trying to breathe. Attacks are triggered by an allergic reaction to food, medication, pollen, or insect stings. The attacks can also be brought on by physical activity or emotional distress. Asthma victims are usually armed with medication to control an attack. Young people should be carrying that medication with them, especially on a trip.

What About AIDS?

Will you be infected with AIDS if you give first aid to a person who is HIV positive? How do you know if a person is carrying the HIV virus when you are preparing to administer first aid?

AIDS stands for acquired immunodeficiency syndrome. It is caused by the human immunodeficiency virus (HIV). When the virus gets into the body, it damages the immune system that fights infection. The virus enters the body in three basic ways: 1) through direct contact with the bloodstream;

2) through the mucous membranes lining the eyes, mouth, throat, rectum, and vagina; and 3) through the womb, birth canal, or breast milk.

The virus cannot enter through the skin unless it is cut or broken at the point of contact. Even then, the possibility of infection is very low unless there is direct contact for a lengthy period of time. Saliva is not known to transmit HIV.

■ The likelihood of HIV transmission during a first aid situation is very low. You are most likely to give first aid to someone you know. Always give care in ways that protect you and the victim from disease transmission.

■ If possible, wash your hands before and after giving care, even if you wear gloves.

■ Avoid touching or being splashed by another person's body fluids, especially blood.

■ Avoid eating and drinking or touching your mouth, eyes, or nose while providing care, or before you wash your hands.

■ Avoid touching objects that may have been contaminated with blood.

■ Avoid handling any of your personal items such as combs or keys while providing care, or before washing your hands.

■ Be prepared with a first aid kit that includes waterless antiseptic hand cleaners and disposable gloves.

Stocking Your First Aid Kit

Bandages, Dressings, and Other Items
■ sterile gauze pads in a variety of 2x2- and 4x4-inch pads

■ rolled gauze: Kling or Kerflex

■ nonstick dressing: Telfa pads (coat with antibacterial ointment or petroleum, but change frequently to prevent drying out and adhering to the skin)

- one-inch adhesive tape
- butterfly bandages or Steristrip bandage assortment
- Ace wrap: three-inch-wide bandage
- large compress: use feminine hygiene pads
- assortment of cloth bandages
- moleskin (for the prevention and treatment of blisters)
- triangular bandage (for holding dressings in place, attaching splints, and creating slings)
- hand cleaner

Equipment and Accessories

- tweezers
- needle
- single-sided razor blade
- bandage scissors
- irrigation syringe
- low-reading thermometer
- SAM Splint or wire mesh
- cold pack
- space blanket
- waterproof matches
- emergency phone numbers and money for a phone call
- bee sting kit
- snakebite kit: compress, suction (use a Sawyer Kit)
- dental kit: oil of cloves, cotton pads, wax
- two pairs of latex gloves
- plastic bags
- small flashlight and extra batteries

Medicines and Drugs: Pain Relief Drugs and Topical Applications

Check with all students for any allergic history to any of these drugs.

- Aspirin: mild analgesic; anti-inflammatory, reduces fever; interferes with blood clotting; can cause nausea; don't give to children.
- Motrin: anti-inflammatory and moderate pain relief;

may cause stomach irritation and nausea.

- Tylenol: for relief of minor to moderate pain such as muscle ache and inflammation; may cause liver damage in excessive doses; first choice for pain relief in many first aid kits.

Allergic Reaction Drugs and Topical Applications

- Benadryl: acts as an antihistamine, sedative, and anti-itch treatment. Use with caution; may cause drowsiness, constipation, weakness, headache, difficulty in urination, diarrhea.

- Ana-Kit: injection of epinephrine and Chlo-Amine tablets to relieve severe allergic reaction. May cause headache, anxiety, heart palpitations.

- Caladryl lotion: a calamine and Benadryl lotion to relieve minor skin irritations.

- Hydrocortisone ointment (2.5 percent): steroid ointment for more severe skin reactions.

Gastrointestinal Medications

- Lomotil: controls diarrhea. Use only if the diarrhea compromises safety or an ability to travel, for it is possible to introduce serious infection and start a fever because of bowel retention.

- Maalox: neutralizes stomach acids and relieves indigestion. Can produce mild diarrhea.

Antibiotic and Antiseptic Ointments

- Neosporin ointment: helps prevent infection in minor cuts and abrasions.

- Betadine: use for topical cleaning of skin around the wound or before lancing a blister. If using to clean a wound, use 25 percent Betadine to 75 percent sterile water. Never use Betadine in a deep wound.

Skin Preparation

- Tincture of Benzoin: prepares skin for application of adhesive.

Other Drugs to Consider

- Cough suppressant: for example, Robitussin cough medicine.

- Decongestant: for example, Afrin nasal spray (not recommended for prolonged periods or for use at high altitudes).
- Antibiotic eyedrops: for example, Neosporin ophthalmic drops.
- Skin care: for example, A and D ointment, which soothes rashes and dry skin. Be sure to check the first aid kit regularly to discard any out-of-date items. Design your first aid to fit your specific activities.

Informing Parents and Supervisors

Parents must know about any injury their son or daughter sustains while under the supervision of the youth ministry. Even small injuries should motivate the youth leader to meet the parents at the 'car when they come to pick up their son or daughter. A quick explanation of what happened and how the injury was treated gives parents information and builds confidence that their young people are being properly supervised.

When the accident is more serious and requires an ambulance or a trip to the emergency room, the parents must be called. It is better for the parents to hear from the youth worker prior to a hospital worker calling to confirm insurance coverage or requesting permission to treat the injury.

There is no subtle or clever way to deliver the news of injury to a parent. Direct and clear is the best style. Don't drag out the information. They want to hear the bottom line: how their son or daughter is right now. Here is a sample conversation:

"Hello, Mrs. Jones, this is Jack Crabtree from the youth ministry down at the church. Please don't be alarmed. I am just calling to tell you that Danny took a fall tonight in the church gym and hurt his arm. He is in good shape, but he is having a lot of pain in that arm. So we decided to bring him to the hospital emergency room for X-rays and treatment. We are here at the hospital right now getting him checked in. I just wanted to let you know what is happening."

That's not too hard! The injury at worst is a broken bone. You would stay on the phone to answer any question the parents would have and give information about how they can find you and come to see their son.

Let's try a harder one: "Hello, Mrs. Collins, this is Jack Crabtree, from the youth ministry bike trip. I am calling to let you know Brian was injured about an hour ago. He took a pretty nasty fall on his bike just outside of Albany. We're at the hospital right now. I don't know the full extent of his injuries, but the ambulance guys told me he is conscious and doing pretty well. He is getting excellent care. The hospital has all the medical information you gave us about Brian, so the doctors will be calling you shortly. I will get off the phone so you can receive that call. Here's the number of the phone I am using to call you. You can call me, or I'll stay on as long as you would like to talk. I'll call you with every piece of news I get from the doctors."

It is very important for the family to know how to contact you. Remember to give them the number of a phone at which you can be reached. Stay calm. Don't raise any speculation about the young person's condition—positive or negative—without solid evidence to support it. Reassure the parents of the care their son or daughter is receiving and of your commitment to keep them informed.

The next call you need to make is to your superior or supervisor in the youth ministry. Give him or her the essential facts about what happened and how you are handling the situation. If you are at a bank of pay phones, use another phone so the parents can call back and get through to you (a mother or father will often call back immediately after calling his or her spouse). Your youth ministry superior can help you think through what you are doing and any logistic problems you might have. You can pray together for God's hand to be on everyone involved. Keep the line of communication open with your superior. Even in the simpler situation of a sprain or broken bone, if you take someone to the emergency room it is wise to call your supervisor. He or she can help you think through everything you should do. Discuss with your supervisor beforehand how any accident should be handled.

After any accident and treatment, the youth ministry worker should write (That's right—pencil and paper!) a report describing what happened to cause the injury, what was done at the scene of the accident, and any additional treatment given by a hospital or doctor. Ask any witnesses to the accident to write or give you a verbal statement (write word for word what they say) about what they saw happen.

If the young person stays under your supervision for the days following, keep notes about his or her condition and recovery. Check on the student regularly. Stay in touch with the parents, giving regular reports to them. Call them with the student and ask the parents what they want you to do and how often they want you to call. It is better to call too often than too little. Keep a written record of all the calls. Combine these notes with your notes on the person's condition and submit them to your superior when you return home.

Checking back regularly with the student and the family builds good relations and provides evidence that you care about what caused the student's injury. Feeling forgotten or ignored angers parents and stimulates lawsuits.

Within a couple weeks, review the entire situation with your supervisor to debrief what happened, how you responded, and what lasting impact will be felt in the ministry. Make this a learning experience to sharpen your safety procedures and first aid response. You might want to institute some new training for your workers or change how a certain event is conducted. The whole process will make your youth ministry safer.

ELEVEN

When the Worst Happens

■ ■

The worst day of my life was Monday, August 20, 1990. We were halfway through our YFC/Campus Life bicycle tour with fifty students and staff riding round trip from Long Island, N.Y., to Maine. This day's outing was a light ride to Ogunquit, Maine, (twenty miles each way) for a fun day at the ocean.

We never made it to the beach. As the adult leader, I was riding in the next-to-last spot in the single file line of eight bikers. My experienced college-age leader was in front, leading the way. I was doing my job, reminding the riders about being careful and warning them about the traffic approaching from behind.

Suddenly Kim Masterson, one of the young women riding in the middle of our single file line, lost her balance and began to fall to her left into the road. The more she fought to regain her balance, the deeper her bike veered into the traffic. Everything seemed to go into slow motion as we watched a vehicle collide with Kim. That sequence is still a clear picture in my mind even though over seven years have passed.

I jumped from my bike and rushed to Kim, who was lying on the road. Checking her vital signs, I could not detect any indication of life. A doctor at the hospital would later confirm that she had died instantly from massive multiple traumas. In the midst of indescribable chaos, I quickly checked to see if anyone else in the group had been injured and organized them to call an ambulance, stop the traffic, and begin helping me.

I quickly prayed for Kim and asked God to give me the strength and wisdom I needed for that moment. I began rescue breathing and CPR while trying to control the bleeding and other apparent injuries in an attempt to give Kim every chance I could to restore her vital signs. The ambulance crew arrived within fifteen minutes and took over the treatment.

While I attended to Kim, the junior leader had found a motorist with a car phone to call the emergency number. The traffic had stopped in both directions. I remember seeing women leave their cars to come to the aid of the students in our group. The students who had not been assigned a job were shaking and crying. These ladies embraced these young people and comforted them as the emergency procedures continued. One of our guys ran back up the road to stop the next approaching bike group. I had told him to keep them at least two hundred feet away from the scene.

When Kim was placed in the ambulance, a police detective asked me to ride with him to the hospital. I quickly ran back to the bike group leaders who had been sitting in hushed silence two hundred feet away and gave them instructions to work out all the necessary logistics. The police were outstanding in the way they helped us solve all the problems this accident presented. On the way to the hospital, I spotted our support van sitting in the stalled traffic. When I stepped out of the police car, their worst fears were confirmed. From the files in the van, I pulled all the information we had on Kim to take with me to the hospital. The staff in the van were given clearance to move ahead and work with the police to help the remaining bikers.

My head was spinning. My heart was breaking. I stiffened every part of my insides to try and maintain control of myself. At the hospital the confirmation of Kim's death came quickly. In nineteen years of youth work, I had always prayed to never be in a hospital room and hear those words. The impact of what Kim's death would mean to her family and everyone involved began to hit me hard.

I was driven to the police station where we started the paperwork and the process of contacting Kim's parents back on Long Island. I called their pastor with the news. He traveled with the Long Island police (who had been contacted by the Maine police) to the parents' place of business. They delivered the bad news to Kim's mom and dad and then called me at the Maine police station. I had always chided kids on previous trips when I warned them about safety, telling them I would not know what to say if I ever had to call their parents. It was even more difficult than I had expected. The police sergeant stood beside me and coached me through the call. Kim's parents were so thoughtful in their shock and grief to express their concern for me and everyone on the trip.

My next calls were to the Long Island YFC office, our local board chairman, and my wife. They started the process of informing the national YFC office and all the parents of students on the trip. While I was calling Long Island, the police sergeant was contacting a local youth agency to request help for our group.

This was a key moment in the whole process. I would have never thought of requesting such help, especially from a secular agency. I needed plenty of help, but the emotional tidal wave sweeping over me hindered my ability to function rationally to determine what needed to be done. I was already experiencing a "walking shock" and was in no position to do any more than I had already been trained to do. The police sergeant had taken me through his part of the process and now had the compassion and foresight to pass me on to the people who could help me face the problems still ahead.

Response to Sudden Death

At this point the focus of this story shifts from the accident to the response of a team of counselors from a variety of agencies who came together to provide emergency care for us. Their response provides a model for helping youth groups who have experienced a sudden death or a severe injury while on a trip away from home.

Within an hour of making the phone calls, I was in a local hospital meeting with a team of six mental health care workers and counselors. They were prepared to help me develop a plan to take the news of Kim's death back to our group. All the students and staff had been returned by bus to the youth home where we had stayed the previous night. They helped me plan the logistics of canceling the trip and returning home. The team spent the first hour of the meeting drawing information from me to understand the special counseling needs our students would require during the twenty-four hours before we traveled home. The coordinator of the team showed great sensitivity toward our Christian faith. One of the people they selected for the team was from a local Christian counseling center. The fact that he had served as a YFC director some years prior helped the other workers understand our group. All of them showed generous love and care for me and the burdens I carried during those hours.

The police called ahead before returning me to the youth home where all the students and staff were waiting for some word from me about Kim. They arranged a quick entrance into the building for me and an immediate meeting with half of the staff and some of Kim's closest friends. After meeting with them, we met with the rest of the staff and finally gathered the whole group to break the news. The team of counselors accompanied me and coached me as I delivered the bad news in each session. They spread themselves among the staff and young people and helped them to talk about their feelings.

For nineteen hours (from 4 p.m. until 11 a.m. the next morning when we boarded the chartered bus) the team of counselors from local agencies were on site with us, available to talk and comfort anyone who needed help. The team broke our group into significant subgroups according to the impact of the accident on each person. They assigned counselors to each group and responded accordingly to the needs they observed.

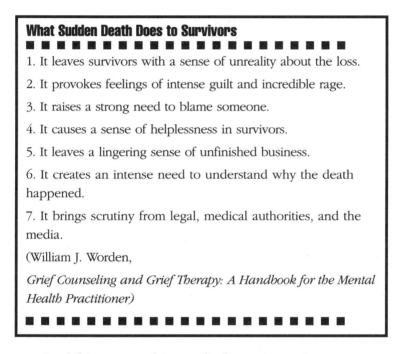

What Sudden Death Does to Survivors

■ ■ ■ ■ ■ ■ ■ ■ ■ ■ ■ ■ ■ ■ ■ ■ ■ ■ ■

1. It leaves survivors with a sense of unreality about the loss.

2. It provokes feelings of intense guilt and incredible rage.

3. It raises a strong need to blame someone.

4. It causes a sense of helplessness in survivors.

5. It leaves a lingering sense of unfinished business.

6. It creates an intense need to understand why the death happened.

7. It brings scrutiny from legal, medical authorities, and the media.

(William J. Worden,

Grief Counseling and Grief Therapy: A Handbook for the Mental Health Practitioner)

■ ■ ■ ■ ■ ■ ■ ■ ■ ■ ■ ■ ■ ■ ■ ■ ■ ■ ■ ■

Our biking group (seven of us) met in a private room with the team coordinator to discuss what had happened to us. This group was the most deeply traumatized because we had seen the accident and been present through the emergency efforts. The counselor asked us to agree to talk about what we had seen only within our group. There was no need for others on the trip to know the details of the tragedy we had witnessed firsthand. We were then asked to share in full detail what we saw happen that morning. It was hard for everyone to speak aloud. Earlier a woman at the police department had given me six large teddy bears to give to any of Kim's special friends. At the time I thought the gift was totally inappropriate, but at the counselor's suggestion I distributed them in our group. Having something soft to hold and squeeze seemed to help some people get out the words and the tears.

When I shared with the group, my whole body shook uncontrollably as I described what I saw and did at the scene of the accident. Later that night when I struggled to stay awake (I was afraid of having a nightmare), I wandered into the dining room and spoke with a counselor. Half of our group stayed up most of the night talking, playing board games, and spending time with the counselors. As much as I hated it, talking about the details did bring some relief.

The next morning we had a large group meeting with some singing and testimonies about Kim and her strong Christian faith. We concluded with a short talk about what the Bible says about death and what happened to Kim when she died.

The counseling team stayed with us until we were loaded on the bus. They gave instruction to us about what we would experience in the days ahead. They helped us realize that our intense feelings were quite normal. It felt like leaving special friends when we said goodbye.

It was a seven-hour bus ride home. While our emotions had been drained during the twenty-four hours in Maine, we were greeted by parents and friends who were bursting with emotion. Every family situation was highly charged with a variety of feelings. No one could escape what had happened to us. The wake (viewing) and the funeral the next three days were a roller coaster of feelings and experiences. We were drawing on our Christian faith for all it could provide. At the same time we were having feelings and thoughts that were entirely different than any we had ever known in the past. Kim's parents greeted us lovingly and showed great concern for our needs. Their support and kindness buoyed our YFC staff.

The night after the funeral, we held an open house at a local church for any student or parent who wanted to attend. Counselors from a local hospital who specialized in assisting victims of trauma volunteered their services. The next few Friday nights, we gathered many students from the trip together for times of games, music, snacks, and talk.

After Kim's funeral the group most resistant to counseling was the staff. We had several all-staff sessions where the counselors found it very difficult to get the staff members to share their feelings. We stopped after two sessions at the request of the staff. I personally went to a counselor weekly for four months and felt the benefit of opening up with him.

Common Progression of Feelings When Reacting to a Death or Disabling Injury

■ ■

1. High anxiety/emotional shock—not in touch with feelings

2. Denial—this can't be happening

3. Anger—strong emotional reactions of all types from screaming to depression; person is less capable of handling any extra pressure

4. Remorse (bargaining)—"If only I had done this…"

5. Grief—dealing with the loss, saying goodbye, and preparing to move on

6. Reconciliation (acceptance, ready to move on)— "Okay, this happened, I'll find a way to deal with it and move ahead with my life.")

■ ■

For all my experience in planning bike trips, I had never considered a contingency plan for a death or serious injury. I would never have considered how a team of local counselors could help our group. They helped us release our thoughts and emotions with their quiet, listening style. Our staff was supported by these professionals and was taught how to respond to a sudden death. In less than twenty-four hours they gave us a foundation from which we could step off into the grieving process. The team of trauma counselors who met with us when we returned home helped us handle our feelings about the funeral and the tensions we felt when we reentered our families. Each group played a special role at a crucial time. Some staff and students took advantage of their services; others did not. It was important to have these services available.

How the Counseling Teams Helped Our Group

They helped the leader by
- providing practical help and emotional support.
- coordinating logistics (arranged food, buses, phone calls).
- formulating a twenty-four hour plan.
- providing personal counseling.

They prepared a counseling strategy by
- dividing people into groups according to the level of trauma.
- taking leadership with each of the groups.
- devising a strategy to break the news sensitively to the group.
- responding to special people and their needs.

They educated the staff by
- helping them deal with their own grief.
- teaching them how to help others handle their grief.
- telling them what to expect in the days and weeks ahead.

Preparing for Traumatic Situations

Obviously no one knows when a tragedy will strike his or her group. The responsibility of the leader is to provide emergency preparedness for the youth ministry staff and the youth of the church. It's normal not to seek help until you need it, but it is wise to be prepared for the worst. Emergency preparedness does not only apply to accidental deaths, but also to suicides and disabling injuries that might occur in the group.

Who Can Help Us Respond?

Which hospital in your area has a trauma team? Familiarize yourself with their services. Keep their phone number and contact names in your personal records and in the church records.

The key person to find is a competent trauma team co-ordinator. This person should know how to respond and should be aware of the resources in the community. The youth group leader cannot put all the pieces of logistics, counseling, and response together when he or she is part of the tragedy. Plan ahead by identifying several people in your community who could fill that role.

Other sources of help include

■ hot lines: Keep a list of contacts and specific specialty services they offer.

■ police, fire, and emergency squads: They offer not only immediate assistance, but they also know additional community resources who can help.

■ organizations such as Compassionate Friends and Survivor Groups: Check their listings in the phone book.

■ prayer chains: What churches in your area have active prayer organizations that can quickly mobilize people to pray for a traumatic situation? Keep their phone numbers readily available.

- therapists and counselors: Who in your community is trained and willing to help in an emergency?
- ministers: Who in your community is trained or experienced in counseling people through grief and trauma? Compile a list.
- health care professionals on church or organization boards: These people are close to ministry and have professional skills to offer.
- bereavement groups: Where can students and staff find long-term support?

Prepare to Educate Students and Staff

Given the probability of some traumatic event happening to your youth group or a student in your group, it is good planning to prepare an information sheet on what they can expect to experience. This sheet can be given to them at the appropriate time with the verbal counseling you or a professional counselor will provide. Here's a sample.

Traumatic Event Stress Information Sheet

You have experienced a traumatic event. Even though the event may be over, you may still be experiencing strong emotional or physical reactions. It is very common and quite normal for people to experience a stress reaction or emotional aftershocks. These aftershocks can appear immediately or be delayed over a wide period of time.

The signs and symptoms of a stress reaction or emotional aftershock may last any length of time depending on the severity of the trauma you experienced. Sometimes just having the understanding and support of caring friends can help you through the stress reaction. Other times the traumatic event can be so strong that you may need to talk with a professional counselor. It doesn't mean you are crazy or weak. What you experienced is just more than one person can handle.

Here are common signs and signals of a stress reaction:

Feelings

- anxiety
- guilt
- grief
- denial
- emotional shock
- fear
- uncertainty
- loss of emotional control
- depression
- feeling overwhelmed
- intense anger
- irritable

Thoughts

- blaming someone/yourself
- confusion
- poor attention
- poor decisions
- poor concentration
- change in alertness
- memory problems
- poor problem solving
- disorientation
- disturbed thinking
- nightmares

Physical

- fatigue
- nausea
- muscles tremors
- twitches
- chest pain*
- difficult breathing*
- elevated blood pressure
- profuse sweating
- fainting
- rapid heartbeat
- thirst
- headaches
- vomiting
- grinding of teeth
- weakness
- dizziness
- chills

*seek immediate medical treatment

Behavior

- withdrawal
- inability to rest

- emotional outbursts
- change in usual habits of communication
- change in appetite
- pacing
- suspiciousness
- hyperalert to environment
- increased alcohol consumption
- easily startled
- erratic movements
- panic or anxiety attacks

How to Deal With Emotional Aftershock

- Within the first twenty-four to forty-eight hours, perform some strenuous physical exercise alternated with relaxation.
- Structure your time and keep busy.
- Realize you are normal and your reactions are normal.
- Talk to people. Talking is the most healing medicine.
- Don't try to numb your pain with drugs or alcohol.
- Reach out to people who are trying to help you.
- Maintain a normal schedule.
- Spend time with others.
- Keep a journal and write your way through the sleepless hours.
- Don't make any big decisions.
- Get plenty of rest.
- Accept recurring thoughts, dreams, and flashbacks as normal. Don't fight them. They will decrease over time and become less painful.
- Eat well-balanced and regular meals (even when you don't feel like it).
- Share your feelings and thoughts with others.

> **Biblical Passages of Hope and Assurance**
> ■ ■ ■ ■ ■ ■ ■
> Psalm 3:1-7
> Isaiah 40:31
> Jeremiah 29:11
> Romans 5:2-5
> 2 Corinthians 4:18-5:8
> ■ ■ ■ ■ ■ ■ ■

Helping a Friend or Family Member Go Through Emotional Aftershock

- Listen carefully.

- Spend time with the person.
- Offer assistance and a listening ear.
- Reassure the person that he or she is safe.
- Help with everyday tasks.
- Give the person some private time.
- Don't take the affected person's anger or other feelings personally.
- Don't tell the person that he or she was "lucky it wasn't worse." Traumatized people are not consoled by such statements.
- Tell the person you are sorry the event happened and that you want to understand and assist him or her.
- Remind the person that confusing emotions are normal.
- Don't attempt to impose your explanation on why the event happened.
- Don't tell the person you know how it feels. You probably don't.
- Be willing to say nothing. Just being there is often the best help you can give.
- Go to any meetings or appointments that concern the event. Offer to go and support him or her.
- Don't ask for details of the trauma. If the person wants to talk, just listen. Let him or her know you are there and you care. It isn't necessary to try and make things better. Offer to pray with them and for them.
- Read passages of assurance and hope from the Bible.

Dealing With a Suicide in or Near Your Group

The friends and family of a person who commits suicide go through a similar bereavement process. They are overwhelmed by the intensity of their feelings. They often feel very angry at the person for ending his or her life. There is guilt and remorse over what should have been done to help the person. They recognize calls for help that they overlooked prior to the suicide. The survivors often feel hopeless and depressed.

Dealing with the survivors starts with encouraging them to express their feelings. Provide places to talk and comfortable ways to bring up the subject. Teach the survivors about the grief process so they can understand that their feelings are normal. Help them call upon their faith in God. Stress God's plan and purpose for them. Encourage them to participate in a weekly support group for several months or more. If necessary, arrange for them to seek professional help.

Dealing With a Disabling Injury

Some people believe that a disabling injury is even more stressful than a death because of the long-term impact it has on the lives of everyone involved. The shock of such an injury is similar to what people feel when someone is killed. The last step of the grieving process is reconciling to the new situation and deciding to move ahead. A disabled person and the family have to go through the same process to reach that conclusion.

There are increasing numbers of books and helpful training classes to assist people in reacting to such injuries and adjusting to living productive lives. Support groups of people who have had similar experiences are available to friends and family members to provide a place to vent their feelings and frustrations.

Returning to "Normal"

After a death or a disabling injury, it is almost impossible to return to ministry the way it was before the event. Spiritually, the best place to start is where the group finds itself. The lessons can be refocused to give attention to the issues raised by the accident. The format of the ministry should include more opportunities for open and honest sharing. When the awkward moments come, just acknowledge how everyone is feeling, and move ahead with a positive statement about the person and what the group has been through. The goal is to help everyone reconcile to the fact of the accident and move forward. The example of the leader can set the tone for the group. If the leader acknowledges his or her need for help, seeks counseling, and talks openly about what happened, it helps the attitude of the whole group.

Nothing to Hide

■ ■

After a fatal accident or any type of serious injury, the leader must immediately file a written report detailing everything that happened before, during, and after the incident. Be sure to list any other witnesses and obtain statements from them. This should be done within seven days of the incident, while the events are still clear in their minds. File these reports with your governing board or supervisor for safekeeping. The police also will be asking for statements from the leader and all witnesses. Warn the young people involved and their families to be very careful about speaking to the media. Usually it is best to refuse comment.

If you become the subject of a lawsuit, secure legal counsel. Your church or organization can help you respond appropriately. If you are properly insured, your legal defense will be covered by the insurance carrier. Do not make any statements about the matter to the public or the media. Conduct yourself with honesty and integrity, remembering the pain and suffering being experienced by the person bringing the suit.

■ ■

Can you return to the same activity or location of the accident? We were encouraged by Kim's parents to continue our bike trips. Their vocal support made it a much easier decision. We re-examined our safety procedures and committed ourselves to continue our high standards of safety. Since the accident, we have conducted two long trips without incident. Approximately half of the students who were on the trip when the accident occurred have ridden with us again. We have tried to create an atmosphere where we can talk about our fears and feelings openly. We're moving ahead. It's been a real-life lesson in overcoming fear.

I hope you won't ever have a young person killed during one of your youth ministry activities. Hopefully my story has motivated you to commit your best efforts to protecting the health and safety of your students. If, despite your best efforts, a student is killed or disabled, I hope this account provides an outline for dealing with the tragedy. You can be confident that God will provide the strength you need in those trying moments.

TWELVE

"Dear Lord, Guard and Protect Us"

■ ■

How safety conscious was Jesus? Imagine his reaction if one of his disciples had the courage to speak up when Jesus was inviting Peter to step off the edge of the boat and on to the water. "Excuse me, Jesus, shouldn't Peter be wearing a personal flotation device approved by the Roman Legion Coast Guard?"

Does being strong on safety practices contradict the life of faith we are trying to live? Should safety procedures and practices be a big concern to us if we are strong in prayer, believe the Bible, and are led by the Spirit?

For many youth workers, the subjects of safety and spirituality pose no contradictions. It's not either/or; it's both/and. But for those in youth work who do hold on to faith and prayer as their only line of safety and to those others who hide their lazy safety habits behind a theological screen, here are six often asked questions.

Does Living by Faith Mean Taking Safety Risks?

Praying prayers of faith and practicing common sense don't contradict each other. A mature Christian seeks to develop a growing, integrated package of common sense, spirituality, and wisdom. Even though we build our youth ministry on God's Word and prayer, we don't need a Bible passage or a prayer session to convince us that we need to wear a life jacket in deep, fast water. God is good. He gave us a brain to handle some of the obvious choices of daily life.

A secular man and a spiritual man standing on the bank of the river deciding if their respective youth groups should go in the water should reach the same conclusion. The spiritual man hasn't demonstrated any lack of faith by deciding not to canoe the river. In fact, the spiritual man has even better reasons for his decision than the secular man who operates strictly on a common-sense basis.

The spiritual man has the benefit of knowing that the lives under his responsibility are special, unique creations of God. He recognizes the fallen world as a dangerous place with pain, suffering, and death caused by rebellion against God. He lives his life to glorify God and to reflect the character of God to everyone he contacts. He realizes handling young lives carelessly does not reflect the character of God.

Can't God Protect Us? Why Should We Try to Protect Ourselves?

Some people argue that the Christian life is built on putting our trust in God alone, not by following the conventions of human beings. Therefore, they say, the Christian youth program operating by faith can take risks because God will guide and protect.

Don't believe it! God is capable of rescuing people from any hazardous situation, but that does not mean we should tempt him or defy the forces of nature. In the desert, Satan challenged Jesus to throw himself off the top on the temple because God would provide angels to catch him. Jesus replied, "It is written 'Do not put the Lord your God to the test.'" Conducting youth ministry without a safety plan and depending on God solely to protect us is putting God to the test. That's not faith—it's foolishness.

Will God protect us when we don't plan for safety or use common sense? That's the wrong question. The real question is, "Are we wise, or are we foolish?"

"He who trusts in himself is a fool, but he who walks in wisdom is kept safe" (Proverbs 28:26).

What does it mean to walk in wisdom?

1. To trust and honor God.
2. To know what God has said in his Word.
3. To make right choices.
4. To learn from our mistakes.

The spiritual, safety-conscious youth leader walks in wisdom. Prayer is central along with learning what God wants us to know from the lessons of life. From our experiences we develop common sense. When you reflect God's character and values, safety becomes a strong motivation. We plan for safety because every young life is valued and treasured by God. If God cares for our young people, shouldn't we use every ounce of our ability to do the same? How could any young person believe he or she is loved by God when at the same time youth ministry leaders who represent God to their students are putting them in dangerous situations with little regard for their safety?

The wise youth worker prays diligently about the safety of his or her students, calling on God to point out what needs to be done to protect each young person. This leader learns from his or her own mistakes and by listening to others. He or she sets aside pride and ego to gain a teachable attitude. Reading this book provides youth workers with true-life stories from which lessons can be learned. Being wise means learning lessons and applying them to the way we live.

Can't We Just Pray and Go for It?

I was speaking at a youth workers training session during the initial stages of preparing the material for this book. I shared with the group the story of Larry (see chapter one), the youth director who had to decide if he would take his youth group canoeing in a swollen river. I paused just before revealing Larry's decision and asked the eighty-five youth leaders what they would do.

One lively, strapping guy said, "I'd get those kids out of the van. We'd have some serious prayer time and then go for it." The other leaders exploded with response. Half seemed energized by his spiritual enthusiasm and confidence that God hears prayers and watches over his children when they step out in faith. The other half seemed shocked at the suggestion of exposing young people to such an obvious risk.

The questions bounced off the walls. What kind of serious prayer session does it take to get inexperienced canoeists safely down a swollen river? How do you know if your prayer time has been serious enough? Does serious prayer mean talking loud and long to God or listening quietly and carefully to God? One leader in the training session wanted to know if this were really a serious prayer session, wouldn't God tell someone in that circle that it wasn't safe for them to be in the river?

We misunderstand prayer when we treat it like a magic insurance policy. We can't do whatever we want and expect God to protect us just because we got two or three to agree in Jesus' name. This is a fundamental issue of prayer. Do we pray to tell God what we want him to do for us, or are we supposed to be listening for some indication of what he wants us to do for him?

The right kind of prayer for a leader to pray sounds something like this: "Lord, as we lead this youth ministry, point out to us what is ungodly, unproductive, and unsafe. Show us how to change it so we will take care of these young people the way you would and be a better witness for your name."

How Can Safety Be a Witness for Jesus?

In the scores of interviews conducted with youth ministry leaders for this book, there was always a "part two" with every accident story they told. What was their future relationship with the student and the family after the incident? Many told us of students and parents turned off to the Church and the Christian faith when they felt the youth ministry had put them (or their child) in jeopardy.

The students who were betrayed sexually or abused physically had the most severe reaction to their leaders. Many of them sunk into deep rebellion against God and doubted the sincerity of any Christian leader. Those who were hurt physically during ministry activities were more forgiving. But in situations where the parents felt the youth leaders were careless or too nonchalant about safety, the walls went up between the youth ministry and the whole family.

All of us in youth ministry staff need to hear Jesus' warning with fresh ears: "But if anyone causes one of these little ones who believe in me to sin, it would be better for him to have a large millstone hung around his neck and to be drowned in the depths of the sea" (Matthew 18:6). God will drop the hammer on those who seduce and abuse kids sexually and physically. It is also justified to extend this warning to youth leaders who harden the hearts of young people and parents toward God because of youth ministry incidents that lacked care and responsibility.

Safety is a positive example to young people and especially to their parents. If you are attempting to be an example of Christ to an unchurched family, one of the very best ways to create interest and involvement is to demonstrate how much you care for their children. In twenty years of leading bike trips, I have seen parents positively impacted for Christ because they saw dedicated concern and care for their teenager by our adult leaders. The skill and professionalism we demonstrated through the discipline of the trip and the care provided when their young person was ill or injured won the admiration and interest of the parents.

All the young people in our groups are precious resources

entrusted to us by God (and their parents) for care and handling. How we treat them shapes their lives. We cannot accept any policy of safety that treats kids less safely than their parents would treat them. Living up to God's treatment standards is even more challenging.

Maybe Accidents and Injuries Are God's Will

Another leader at the training session raised the question, "Whatever happened to the sovereignty of God? We can't be worrying about everything that might happen to our kids. What's wrong with just trusting that whatever happens is the will of God?" Are we trying to do God's job by being so paranoid about safety?

When Kim Masterson was killed on our bicycle trip, I asked a thousand "what if" and "why" questions. The original plan for the trip had us riding on that stretch of road the day before the actual accident. It poured heavy rain that day. We had an extra day on our schedule and made the decision not to put ourselves on the road in those conditions. The day of the accident was bright and sunny. If we had ridden the previous day in the rain and had taken the sunny day off, would we have avoided the accident and Kim's death? Kim was a last minute registrant on the trip, headed for her freshman year of college as soon as she returned home. If she had been home preparing for college on that day, would she have died in different circumstances? Had God appointed that day as her last day on earth? Was it God's will for Kim to die on that day on a road in Maine? I don't think I'll ever know the answers to those questions while I am alive on this earth.

I do have great confidence in the sovereignty of God. I believe that God works out all things for our good. It doesn't mean that everything that happens to us is good. The evil in our fallen world produces an environment that includes pain, suffering, and death. What is remarkable is God's ability to use even these terrible events for our long-term good. In our hedonist world, I need a constant reminder that God is not working to make me happy, but to fulfill his purpose.

Yet my confidence in the sovereignty of God is no reason to relax my best human efforts to keep everyone on a bicycle trip safe from danger. Life is precious, and my job (both inside and outside of youth ministry) is to protect it.

I challenge those who would argue the sovereignty of God as a reason for not giving our best effort for safety. Do you leave your house unlocked and believe that if it is God's will for your house to be robbed, it will happen regardless of what precautions you might take? Most people don't! They trust God to provide protection, but they do their part by installing and using locks on the doors to keep their cars and houses from being burglarized.

It is more than just common sense to recognize the dangers of this world and respond appropriately. If we love our money and our valuables and take steps to protect them, can we say we love young people when we don't take even more precautions to protect the ones God has placed in our care? We recognize the dangers and observe safety procedures because we don't want to lose any of them. Our safety efforts in youth ministry should not be any different than what we practice with our most precious material possessions.

We live in a fallen world. It is governed by physical laws and natural forces. We plan our steps according to those forces. Although God is both capable and caring, you can't plan your youth ministry with the expectation that God will suspend the laws of physics or the force of gravity when you shoot up a 911 prayer.

God gave us the task (and responsibility) of dominating the earth. Part of that task requires us to familiarize ourselves with how the world works and to teach ourselves and others how to respond. We learn about our environment and stay away from dangerous activities. Even strong Christians don't hold a prayer service in the middle of a lake holding up a large metal cross during a thunderstorm.

When Accidents Happen, Has God Failed Us?

A friend told me I shouldn't be praying for safety in front of the students in our youth group. She is concerned that students might lose faith in God's ability to answer our prayers if we have an accident and someone is hurt or killed.

If an accident happens, does it mean God didn't hear our prayers for safety? Perhaps we should thank God that nothing worse happened to our group. Maybe we were shielded from seeing how God protected us from a greater disaster. Perhaps we are guilty of taking for granted all the instances of God's protection each day that we don't see. We need to keep praying with intensity for God's hand to be on all we do.

After an accident some students and staff may feel strongly that God doesn't care. When Job struggled through his calamities, he learned that it's not always possible to understand the reasons why they occurred. Sometimes the answers and explanations are held back. Believing in God or prayer does not protect us from trouble. Rather, it prepares us to handle what life in a fallen world brings to us. The message of Job is not to give up. God may allow suffering in our lives for reasons we can't understand. Through the whole process our faith and trust in God can grow.

Jay Kesler, president of Taylor University, has said when we see some tragic accident happen we have three choices: 1) We can believe there is no God; 2) we can believe God causes these things to happen; or 3) we can understand that God allows these things to happen without causing them. God has created a physical universe with natural laws that govern how we live. Sometimes gravity saves a person's life;

other times gravity pulls a person to his or her death. Everything we know about God tells us that when accidents happen, God is as sad about the injuries or deaths as the people who are involved.

Final Thoughts

For people to believe the message of God's love, they must trust the messenger. God has placed youth ministers in a strategic position to change the lives of entire families. Their mission begins with trust. If parents and students know the youth ministry staff care so much for them that its top priority is to protect their safety, they will be open to the message it brings. Lack of planning and care for safety is not only criminal, it is a terrible witness for Christ.

Attention to safety concerns brings glory to the name of Christ. It shows love and concern. It lays the foundation for future trust when the life-changing message of Jesus is presented. Safety concerns are not a contradiction to a life of faith. In youth ministry, safety concerns open the door for people to discover a life of faith.

Sample Health Form

_____

(Name of Church or Youth Ministry)

(Please Print)

Name of Student_____ Date of Birth_____

Address _____ Age_____

Town _____State _____ Zip_____

Phone Number (___) _____ Sex _____ Height_____

Weight _____ Social Security Number_____

Emergency Contact Person:

Parent/Guardian Name_____

Address (if different from student)

_____

Town _____State _____ Zip_____

Phone Number (Home) (____) _____

(Work) (____) _____

Alternate Contact Person: (Use someone near the primary contact)

Name _____

Address

_____

Town _____State _____ Zip_____

Phone Number (Home) (____) _____

(Work) (____) _____

If you have medical insurance, your carrier will be billed for medical charges in the case of illness or injury while your child is at the activity.

Do you have health insurance? _____ Yes _____ No

Name of Insurance Company

_____

Policy Number_____
Group Number _____
In whose name is the insurance?

_____

Family Doctor _____ City/Town _____
Phone Number _____

If your child should require medical attention for injuries received or illnesses contracted prior to activity, please send us the necessary information to give him/her proper medical care during his/her time with the youth ministry activity.

Health History:
Pre-existing or present medical conditions

_____

_____

Name and dosage of any medications that must be taken

_____

Any allergies? _____ to medications? _____

___ Hay Fever ___ Heart Condition ___ Diabetes
___ Insect Stings ___ Epilepsy/Nervous Disorders
___ Asthma ____ Frequent Stomach Upsets
___ Physical Handicap
___ Any major illnesses during the past year?
If any of the above are checked, please give details (i.e., include normal treatment of allergic reactions)

_____

_____

Date of Last Tetanus Shot _____ Contact Lenses? _____
Any swimming restrictions? _____ Yes _____ No
What? _____
Any activity restrictions? _____ Yes _____ No
What? _____

Sample Parent Medical and Liability Release Statement:

I understand that in the event medical intervention is needed, every attempt will be made to contact immediately the persons listed on this form. In the event I cannot be reached in an emergency during the activity dates shown on this form, I hereby give my permission to the physician or dentist selected by the activity leader to hospitalize, to secure medical treatment and/or to order an injection, anesthesia, or surgery for my child as deemed necessary.

I understand that my insurance coverage for my child will be used as primary coverage in the event medical intervention is needed. Coverage by (name of the church or organization) through its accident policy will be used as a backup for what my family's insurance does not cover.

I understand all reasonable safety precautions will be taken at all times by the (name of the church or organization) and its agents during the events and activities. I understand the possibility of unforeseen hazards and know the inherent possibility of risk. I agree not to hold (name of church or organization), its leaders, employees, and volunteer staff liable for damages, losses, diseases, or injuries incurred by the subject of this form.

Parent/Guardian Signature _____

Date _____

Signature of Student (if over 18 years of age)

_____

Sample Parent Information and Release Form

_____
(Name of Church of Youth Ministry)

Parent/Guardian Information and Permission Form

Name of Activity and Dates _____

(Please Print)

Name of Student _____

Date of Birth _____ Age _____

Address _____

Town_____State_____Zip_____

Phone Number (__)_____Sex_____

Sample Student Information and Code of Behavior Agreement

Description of the activity/event and dates (for example):

    What you will be doing

    Departure and return times/locations

    Supervision and free time activities

    Accommodations and curfew times

    How you can be reached by phone

Listed below are some of the activities we have planned to offer to the students during the trip. Place your initials next to specific activities listed below to indicate your approval of your child's participation.

(for example):

_____ horseback riding   _____ playing in sports

_____ rock climbing   _____ swimming in a lake

_____ canoeing   _____ walking the ropes course

_____ participating in   _____ other
     the program

Rules of Behavior Expected of Each Student

(for example)

1. No alcohol or drugs permitted.
2. Attendance at meetings is mandatory.
3. No guys in girls sleeping quarters (vice versa, too).
4. Follow curfew.
5. No smoking.
6. Other _____

Parent and Student Release Statement:

As parent/legal guardian of (name of student), I have reviewed the information about the youth ministry activity/event and give my permission for the subject of this release to be involved in the overall activities and in the specific activities that I have initialed above.

I/We have reviewed the rules of the activity and agree that the subject of this release will abide by them. I/We also acknowledge that if the subject of the release has to return home early for discipline violations, it will be at my/our expense.

I/We consent to the use of any video images, photographs, audio recordings, or any other visual or audio reproduction that may be taken of the subject of this release during the activity/event to be used, distributed, or shown as (name of the church or organization) sees fit.

I/We understand all reasonable safety precautions will be taken at all times by the (name of the church or organization) and its agents during the events and activities. I/We understand the possibility of unforeseen hazards and know the inherent possibility of risk. I/We agree not to hold (name of church or organization), its leaders, employees, and volunteer staff liable for damages, losses, diseases, or injuries incurred by the subject of this form.

Parent/Guardian Signature _____

Student Signature _____

Date _____

Sample Promotional Release Form

Sample Statement:

I, the undersigned, hereby consent to the use of any videotapes, photographs, slides, audiotapes, or any other visual or audio reproduction in which I may appear by (name of the organization). I understand that these materials are being used for promotion of the youth ministry of (name of organization), which includes recruitment and fund-raising efforts.

I release (name of organization) from any liability connected with the use of my picture or voice recording as part of any promotional, recruitment, or fund-raising program.

Date _____

Signed _____

(youth)

Signed _____

(consented to by parent/guardian)

All pictures and recordings should be accounted for and protected from use by any unauthorized person or organization.

(Recently youth organizations have been warned about videotaping their activities for fear that the tapes might end up being shown not on "America's Funniest Home Videos," but rather in a courtroom as evidence in a lawsuit. For details, see the story of ski trip accident caught on video in chapter seven.)

Sample Ministry Vehicle Policy Statement

(Name of Church/Organization)

Vehicle Use Policy Statement

Date Approved

Usage:

Define what groups and staff members can use the vehicle and under what circumstances.

Define what groups and people cannot use the vehicle and under what circumstances.

Designated Drivers (here's one church's specific rules)

It will be the responsibility of the following groups to submit to the vehicle committee prior to September 1st each year their lists of proposed designated drivers.

Designated Drivers Must Meet the Following Qualifications:

1. Licensed driver must be 21 years or older.
2. Driver must be group sponsor/leader of one of the organizations designated to use the vehicle.
3. Driver must have a satisfactory Traffic Violations and Vehicle Accident Record.
4. Driver must sign acknowledgment of "Responsibilities of Designated Driver," which includes an understanding of insurance coverage as it pertains to the driver.
5. Driver must exhibit responsible driving habits.

The vehicle committee shall evaluate and approve designated drivers prior to October 1st each year. Designated drivers shall be noted in the October youth committee meeting minutes and shall be in effect for the period of one year (October 1 to September 30).

The vehicle committee shall have the right to revoke or suspend driver status (for cause) at any time.

Driver Checklist
Vehicle Comittee Checklist
1. Warning to anyone violating the above policies and rules
2. Vehicle logbook
3. State purpose of logbook
4. Who is responsible for keeping logbook
5. Items to appear on logbook report
6. Schedule of maintenance on vehicle
7. Responsibilities of vehicle committee and members
8. Specify who is to do what jobs
9. Sample form for designated drivers to sign

Driver Checklist
Prior to Any Trip (personalize this section)
1. Van pick-up procedure (write the details to fit local use)
2. Use of logbook and trip record sheet
3. Driver submit and sign acknowledgment of driving responsibilities
4. Driver test drives vehicle
5. Use of portable CB radio

Driver Checklist
During the Trip
1. Seat belt regulations
2. Capacity of vehicle rule
3. Obey state traffic laws
4. Drive defensively and carefully

Driver Checklist
After the Trip
1. Refueling and cleaning required
2. Return of vehicle to certain location
3. Reporting of any problems
4. Completion of log sheet/trip report

Acknowledgment of Responsibilities of Designated Driver

I have read and will adhere to the responsibilities governing the use of either church-owned vehicles or personal vehicles while transporting young people to and from church-sponsored activities.

I am aware that automotive insurance liability will generally follow the flow below in the event of an accident, and as such, subject me to certain liability risks.

1. Owner of Vehicle _____

2. Driver of Vehicle _____

3. Church (only in furtherance of church activity) _____

Signature of Driver_____

Date _____

Safety Organizations

American Camping Association
5000 State Road 67 North
Martinsville, IN 46151
(765) 342-8456
www.aca-camps.org

American Heart Association
7272 Greenville Avenue
Dallas, TX 75231
800-AHA-USA1
www.americanheart.org

American Red Cross
811 Gatehouse Road
Falls Church, VA 22042
(703) 206-7090
www.redcross.org

Boy Scouts of America
1325 West Walnut Hill Lane
Irving, TX 75038
(972) 580-2000
www.bsa.scouting.org

Christian Camping International
405 West Rockrimmon Blvd.
Colorado Springs, CO 80919
(719) 260-9400
www.cciusa.org

National Safety Council
1121 Spring Lake Drive
Itasca, IL 60143
(630) 285-1121
www.nsc.org

YMCA of the USA
101 North Wacker Drive
Chicago, IL 60606
(312) 977-0031
www.ymca.net

YWCA of the USA
Empire State Building, Suite 301
350 Fifth Avenue
New York, NY 10118
(212) 273-7800
www.ywca.org

Group Publishing, Inc.
Attention: Product Development
P.O. Box 481
Loveland, CO 80539
Fax: (970) 669-1994

Evaluation for *Better Safe Than Sued*

Please help Group Publishing, Inc., continue to provide innovative and useful resources for ministry. Please take a moment to fill out this evaluation and mail or fax it to us. Thanks!

● ● ●

1. As a whole, this book has been (circle one)

not very helpful   very helpful

1   2   3   4   5   6   7   8   9   10

2. The best things about this book:

3. Ways this book could be improved:

4. Things I will change because of this book:

5. Other books I'd like to see Group publish in the future:

6. Would you be interested in field-testing future Group products and giving us your feedback? If so, please fill in the information below:

Name _____

Street Address _____

City _____ State _____ Zip _____

Phone Number _____ Date _____

Bible Study Series

Give Your Teenagers a Solid Faith Foundation That Lasts a Lifetime!

Here are the *essentials* of the Christian life—core values teenagers *must* believe to make good decisions now...and build an *unshakable* lifelong faith. Developed by youth workers like you...field-tested with *real* youth groups in *real* churches...here's the meat your kids *must* have to grow spiritually—presented in a fun, involving way!

Each 4-session **Core Belief Bible Study Series** book lets you easily...

● Lead deep, compelling, *relevant* discussions your kids won't want to miss...

● Involve teenagers in exploring life-changing truths...

● Help kids create healthy relationships with each other—and you!

Plus you'll make an *eternal difference* in the lives of your kids as you give them a solid faith foundation that stands firm on God's Word.

Here are the Core Belief Bible Study Series titles already available...

Senior High Studies

Why **Authority** Matters	0-7644-0892-5
Why **Being a Christian** Matters	0-7644-0883-6
Why **Creation** Matters	0-7644-0880-1
Why **Forgiveness** Matters	0-7644-0887-9
Why **God** Matters	0-7644-0874-7
Why **God's Justice** Matters	0-7644-0886-0
Why **Jesus Christ** Matters	0-7644-0875-5
Why **Love** Matters	0-7644-0889-5
Why **Our Families** Matter	0-7644-0894-1
Why **Personal Character** Matters	0-7644-0885-2
Why **Prayer** Matters	0-7644-0893-3
Why **Relationships** Matter	0-7644-0896-8
Why **Serving Others** Matters	0-7644-0895-X
Why **Spiritual Growth** Matters	0-7644-0884-4
Why **Suffering** Matters	0-7644-0879-8
Why **the Bible** Matters	0-7644-0882-8
Why **the Church** Matters	0-7644-0890-9
Why **the Holy Spirit** Matters	0-7644-0876-3
Why **the Last Days** Matter	0-7644-0888-7
Why **the Spiritual Realm** Matters	0-7644-0881-X
Why **Worship** Matters	0-7644-0891-7

Junior High/Middle School Studies

The Truth About **Authority**	0-7644-0868-2
The Truth About **Being a Christian**	0-7644-0859-3
The Truth About **Creation**	0-7644-0856-9
The Truth About **Developing Character**	0-7644-0861-5
The Truth About **God**	0-7644-0850-X
The Truth About **God's Justice**	0-7644-0862-3
The Truth About **Jesus Christ**	0-7644-0851-8
The Truth About **Love**	0-7644-0865-8
The Truth About **Our Families**	0-7644-0870-4
The Truth About **Prayer**	0-7644-0869-0
The Truth About **Relationships**	0-7644-0872-0
The Truth About **Serving Others**	0-7644-0871-2
The Truth About **Sin and Forgiveness**	0-7644-0863-1
The Truth About **Spiritual Growth**	0-7644-0860-7
The Truth About **Suffering**	0-7644-0855-0
The Truth About **the Bible**	0-7644-0858-5
The Truth About **the Church**	0-7644-0899-2
The Truth About **the Holy Spirit**	0-7644-0852-6
The Truth About **the Last Days**	0-7644-0864-X
The Truth About **the Spiritual Realm**	0-7644-0857-7
The Truth About **Worship**	0-7644-0867-4

Exciting Resources for Your Youth Ministry

All-Star Games From All-Star Youth Leaders

The ultimate game book—from the biggest names in youth ministry! All-time no-fail favorites from Wayne Rice, Les Christie, Rich Mullins, Tiger McLuen, Darrell Pearson, Dave Stone, Bart Campolo, Steve Fitzhugh, and 21 others! You get all the games you'll need for any situation. Plus, you get practical advice about how to design your own games and tricks for turning a *good* game into a *great* game!

ISBN 0-7644-2020-8

Last Impressions: Unforgettable Closings for Youth Meetings

Make the closing moments of your youth programs powerful and memorable with this collection of Group's best-ever low-prep (or no-prep!) youth meeting closings. You get over 170 favorite closings, each tied to a thought-provoking Bible passage. Great for anyone who works with teenagers!

ISBN 1-55945-629-9

The Youth Worker's Encyclopedia of Bible-Teaching Ideas

Here are the most comprehensive idea-books available for youth workers. With more than 365 creative ideas in each of these 400-page encyclopedias, there's at least one idea for every book of the Bible. You'll find ideas for retreats and overnighters...learning games... adventures...special projects...affirmations...parties...prayers...music... devotions...skits...and more!

Old Testament   ISBN 1-55945-184-X
New Testament ISBN 1-55945-183-1

PointMaker™ Devotions for Youth Ministry

These 45 PointMakers™ help your teenagers discover, understand, and apply biblical principles. Use PointMakers as brief meetings on specific topics or slide them into any youth curriculum to make a lasting impression. Includes handy Scripture and topical indexes that make it quick and easy to select the perfect PointMaker for any lesson you want to teach!

ISBN 0-7644-2003-8

Order today from your local Christian bookstore, or write:
Group Publishing, P.O. Box 485, Loveland, CO 80539.